Trotsky on World War One

All translations except *The War and the International* by **Pete Dickenson**

January 2015

a **socialist party** publication

Trotsky on World War One

ISBN: 978-1-870958-66-7

Published by Socialist Publications

Typeset in Adobe Gramond Pro 10.5 pt and Myriad Pro
Printed by The Russell Press, Basford, Nottingham NG6 0BT

Distribution by Socialist Books,
PO Box 24697, London, E11 1YD
Telephone +44 (0)20 8988 8789
e-mail: bookshop@socialistparty.org.uk
www.socialistbooks.co.uk

typesetting & design: kavita graphics (tu)
dennis@kavitagraphics.co.uk

Contents

Introduction

The Russia Revolutionary Leon Trotsky's very extensive writings on World War I, the vast majority of which have been unavailable in English, contain invaluable lessons for socialists and are also essential reading for those studying the history of the period. The 100th anniversary of the start of a war that Trotsky from the start dubbed imperialist, marks a fitting time to begin the publication or re-publication of his writings from the period. The articles are divided into those written for the socialist press, *Golos* (The Voice) and *Nashe Slovo* (Our Word), followed by the war correspondence mainly for *'Kievskaya Mysl'* (Kieven Thought). Within these subdivisions they are reproduced chronologically. Apart from the first article, *The War and the International*, all the pieces are translated into English for the first time.

The War and the International was Trotsky's most theoretically significant war-time work. It contained the first developed statement from a socialist that put forward an anti-war programme, characterising the war as imperialist and condemning those workers' parties that supported it. Written in Zurich in the first months of the war, it was first published in Russian in November 1917 in the Parisian socialist emigré journal Golos. Shortly afterwards it appeared in German and was circulated in German speaking countries, whose Social Democratic parties were its main targets, because of their leading role in the pre-war international socialist movement. Trotsky's booklet was however accused by all belligerents of bringing succour to their enemies. The most famous piece by Trotsky from this time, the Zimmerwald Manifesto, the declaration by an international meeting of anti-war socialists held in Switzerland in 1915, draws on the ideas in this book. In Chapter 18 of his autobiography, *My Life*, first published in 1930, he comments:

"The booklet, *The War and the International*, like all my other books, had its own peculiar destiny, first in Switzerland, then in Germany and France, later in America, and finally in Soviet Russia. A few words must be said about all this.... From Switzerland it found its way, as early as December, 1914, to Austria and Germany...

Intended for German countries, the pamphlet was directed first of all against the German Social Democracy, the leading party of the Second International. I remember that a journalist named Heilmann, who played first-violin in the orchestra of chauvinism, called my book mad, but quite logical in its madness. I could not have wished for greater praise. There was, of course, no lack of hints that my book was an artful tool of *Entente*[1] propaganda.

Later on, in France, I came unexpectedly across a report in the French papers, by way of Switzerland, that one of the German courts had sentenced me in a state of contumacy to imprisonment for the Zurich pamphlet. From this I concluded that the pamphlet had hit the mark. The Hohenzollern[2] judges did me a very good turn by their sentence, a sentence that I was not in any hurry to serve. For the slanderers and spies of the *Entente*, this German court-sentence was always a stumbling-block in their noble efforts to prove that I was nothing more than an agent of the German general staff.

This did not keep the French authorities, however, from holding up my book at the frontier on the strength of its "German origin".....

After the October revolution, an enterprising New York publisher brought out my German pamphlet as an imposing American book. According to his own statement, President Wilson asked him, by telephone from the White House, to send the proofs of the book to him; at that time, the President was composing his *Fourteen Points*, and, according to reports from people who were informed, could not get over the fact that a Bolshevik had forestalled him in his best formulae. Within two months the sales of the book in America reached 16,000 copies. Then came the days of the Brest-Litovsk peace.[3] The American press raised a furious campaign against me, and the book instantly disappeared from the market.

In the Soviet Republic my Zurich pamphlet had by that time gone through several editions, serving as a text-book for the study of the Marxist attitude toward the war. It disappeared from the "market" of the Communist International only after 1924, the year when "Trotskyism" was discovered. At present, the pamphlet is still under a ban, as it was before the revolution.

Indeed, it would seem that books have their own destiny ..."

In fact, President Wilson lifted several phrases and formulations from Trotsky, including the proposal for a 'United States of Europe'. It is clear though that Wilson's utopian conception of a capitalist united Europe had nothing in common with Trotsky's idea. In the booklet Trotsky writes: " In the present historical conditions the proletariat is not interested in defending an anachronistic national 'Fatherland', which has become the main impediment to economic advance, but in the creation of a new, more powerful and stable fatherland, the republican United States of Europe, as the foundation for the United States of the World. To the imperialist blind alley of capitalism the proletariat can oppose only the socialist organisation of the world economy as the practical programme of the day".

The present publication follows the version in the Marxist Internet Archive. This is based on the uncopyrighted edition by the Wesley Press in 1971, that itself is based on the original English language version called *'The Bolsheviki and World Peace'* published by Boni and Liveright, New York,1918. Use is made here of the end-notes to the Wesley Press edition. Trotsky's notes are in the body of the text and shown in [].

The latter part of the book is a collection of articles by Trotsky on the war previously untranslated into English. They are drawn largely from three journals he was associated with in the period 1914-1916, *Golos* (The Voice), *Nashe Slovo* (Our Word) and *Kievskaya Mysl'* (Kieven Thought).The translations from *Kievskaya Mysl'* are based on the reproductions in Volume 9 of Trotsky's Complete Works, Moscow-Leningrad, 1927, (*L Trotsky, Sochinenya, Tom IX, Moskva-Leningrad, 1927*), other translations are from the original newspapers. Some use is made in the translations here of the end-notes from Volume 9 of the Complete Works. Also, the italicised emphases that were inserted in the Complete Works have been included here. In a brief introduction to Volume 9, Trotsky makes the point that all the articles were written under conditions of military censorship, which sometimes resulted in large blank spaces appearing in *Nashe Slovo*. It may also have been the case that Trotsky could not express his opinions as clearly as he would have wished in what remained of the paper. In the translations here the position of deletions made by the censor are shown in square brackets []. Where the deleted text was subsequently re-inserted in the Complete Works, this is included. In some of the articles in *Nashe Slovo*, there is extensive use of irony. Trotsky throughout his life made very effective use of this literary technique to attack his opponents, but it is laid on with such a thick brush in some of the articles here, that it was probably a device to evade the censorship. It may be significant that in one article where the irony is particularly relentless, *'The National Principle'*, the censor's pen is absent.

Golos was edited in Paris by Julius Martov, a leader of the Menshevik wing of the Russian Social Democracy. (Marxists at the time referred to themselves as Social Democrats). Trotsky was closely politically associated with Martov at the beginning of the war. At this time, both wings of the Social Democracy, Lenin's Bolsheviks and the Mensheviks took a strong anti-war position. In January 1915 *Golos* was suppressed by the French government and a few weeks later Nashe Slovo appeared, under the joint editorship of Martov and Trotsky. (Trotsky had moved from Zurich in Switzerland to Paris in November 1914 to become the Paris-based war correspondent of *Kievskaya*

Mysl', a mainstream pro-war paper published in Kiev). During1915, the Mensheviks adopted a more and more vacillating position on opposition to the war, leading in 1916 to a split between Martov and Trotsky, and the former's departure from the paper.

Nashe Slovo was a daily paper produced by a handful of penniless emigrés, running to 219 editions before suffering the same fate as *Golos* in the autumn of 1916. Trotsky's literary output was prodigious in this period, including his work for *Kievskaya Mysl'*. In *Nashe Slovo* there was a constant battle with the censor, but Trotsky was constrained in a different way when writing for *Kievskaya Mysl'*, since it supported Russia in the war. For this journal, that he relied on for his living, he mainly produced very perceptive surveys and analysis of the military situation as well as brilliant pieces of war reporting. Although not overtly party-political, the informed reader can detect a clear underlying Marxist approach. Trotsky comments in *My Life* that he was able to use the military knowledge acquired researching these articles a few years later as the head of the Red Army.

The articles have been chosen to be representative of the various themes he addressed in his writings, but the emphasis is on the first year of the war. The intention is to eventually translate all Trotsky's output from the First World War, including material from the later years.

The title of the first piece, *Gregus on the Democratic List*, is an ironic reference to a guard called Gregus who tortured political prisoners in the revolution of 1905. The article is mainly an attack on Pavel Miliukov, the most prominent Russian liberal politician of the time, who was claiming that the war was being fought by Tsarism for democratic principles. *In the Balkans* analyses the situation in Romania and Bulgaria, neutral at the time, and the rotten politics of their mainstream capitalist parties. Trotsky had great experience of the region as a correspondent in the Balkan Wars that preceded WW1 and had close links to prominent local Marxists. *'The Home Front'* returns to the attack on the Russian liberals, as does *A Convention of Confusion and Impotence*, the latter contrasting the historical experience of liberalism in France and Russia. In these articles Trotsky also exposes socialists in Russia and France who had taken a pro-war positions. *A Year of War* published on August 4th 1915, is a rousing appeal to the labour movement to oppose the war, and an analysis of the historical developments that led to the war and the collapse of the 2nd International.

The Military Disaster and Political Perspectives considers the reasons for the defeats of the Russian army in the summer of 1915 and comes to the conclusion that the war will be lost. From this Trotsky goes on to argue that defeat will not necessarily lead to revolution, as after the Russo-Japanese war of 1904, and that the revolution does not need an accumulation of defeats. This touches on an important issue of debate among Russian Marxists in this period. (For background see *'The Bolsheviks & the war'*,

Socialism Today, July/August 2014 http://www.socialismtoday.org/180/bolsheviks.html). Trotsky's perspective that the huge scale of the war compared to 1904 would hamstring social developments for a long period, was, like all perspectives, conditional. Perspectives are a necessary working hypothesis, which have to be regularly corrected. For example, Lenin said in 1916 that there wouldn't be a revolution in his lifetime. When the revolutions of 1917 broke out, any apparent differences between the two men evaporated. (Two extracts from this article were published in English in the 1980s by Monad Press, New York).

"The National Principle", in a highly ironic manner, exposes the rank hypocrisy of the belligerent powers, as well as the leaders of the workers parties supporting them, who claimed to stand for the right of nations to self-determination. The final article in this part, *Serb Terrorists and French 'Liberators'. The Mood in Vienna in the first days of the war*, was not published during the war, but research on the text shows it was written in 1916. It is taken from Trotsky's archive. It may not have been published because of problems with the censorship, which was becoming ever more heavy handed during that year.

Articles for the socialist press are followed by a selection of Trotsky's war correspondence. *A Political Moratorium* describes the patriotic sentiment that swept over the Austro-Hungarian empire at the outbreak of war, that pushed aside national and social contradictions. By examining the history of the empire, Trotsky concluded that this situation would be only temporary. *Guerre D'Usure*, (A War of Attrition), written in January 1915, analyses the military developments of the first months of the war, and predicts a bloody stalemate. This was before most other commentators had come to this conclusion. *The 7th Infantry in the Belgium Epic* is a remarkable piece of war reporting covering the German onslaught on Belgium through the eyes of a Belgian soldier. Trotsky is clearly sympathetic to the plight of Belgium, caught in a vice between the major powers, but at the same time he graphically exposes the horror and futility of war.

The material for *The Trench* is based on Trotsky's contacts with Russians who had volunteered for the French army. He very atmospherically re-creates life in the trenches, the tedium, terror and absurdity, without ever being there, since the French military authorities would not give reporters access. Nevertheless he gets inside the minds of the soldiers in a convincing way. This is developed in *Psychological Enigmas of War* that looks at the long-term impact on consciousness of the war and predicts its effect would be felt for decades or longer.

Pete Dickenson. *November 2014.*

Notes

1. The Entente was the alliance that included France, Britain and Russia.
2. Hohenzollern was the family name of the German Kaiser
3. Brest-Litovsk peace, refers to the treaty between Soviet Russia and Germany after the 1917 October Revolution. In it, Russia was forced to temporarily concede large parts of territory.

№ 9. Наше Слово

NOTRE PAROLE

NACHE SLOWO

Ce Journal ne peut être crié

Ликвидація довѣрія.

ОБЗОРЪ ПЕЧАТИ.

ЗАЯВЛЕНІЕ

Достойно отмѣтить.

Соціалистич. хроника.

Nashe Slovo, (Our Word)

Writings for the Socialist Press
The War and the International
Part I.

Author's Preface

The forces of production which capitalism has evolved have outgrown the limits of nation and state. The national state, the present political form, is too narrow for the exploitation of these productive forces. The natural tendency of our economic system, therefore, is to seek to break through the state boundaries. The whole globe, the land and the sea, the surface as well as the interior has become one economic workshop, the different parts of which are inseparably connected with each other. This work was accomplished by capitalism. But in accomplishing it the capitalist states were led to struggle for the subjection of the world-embracing economic system to the profit interests of the bourgeoisie of each country. What the politics of imperialism has demonstrated more than anything else is that the old national state that was created in the revolutions and the wars1 of 1789-1815, 1848-1859, 1864-1866, and 1870 has outlived itself, and is now an intolerable hindrance to economic development.

The present war is at bottom a revolt of the forces of production against the political form of nation and state. It means the collapse of the national state as an independent economic unit.

The nation must continue to exist as a cultural, ideological and psychological fact, but its economic foundation has been pulled from under its feet. All talk of the present bloody clash being a work of national defence is either hypocrisy or blindness. On the contrary, the real, objective significance of the War is the breakdown of the present national economic centres, and the substitution of a world economy in its stead. But the way the governments propose to solve this problem of imperialism is not through the intelligent, organized cooperation of all of humanity's producers, but through the exploitation of the world's economic system by the capitalist class of the victorious country; which country is by this War to be transformed from a Great Power into the World Power.

The War proclaims the downfall of the national state. Yet at the same time it proclaims the downfall of the capitalist system of economy. By means of the national state, capitalism has revolutionized the whole economic system of the world. It has divided the whole earth among the oligarchies of the great powers, around which were grouped the satellites, the small nations, who lived off the rivalry between the great ones. The future development of world economy on the capitalistic basis means a ceaseless struggle for new and ever new fields of capitalist exploitation, which must be obtained from one and the same source, the earth. The economic rivalry under the banner of militarism is accompanied by robbery and destruction which violate the elementary principles of human economy. World production revolts not only against the confusion produced by national and state divisions but also against the capitalist economic organizations, which has now turned into barbarous disorganization and chaos.

The War of 1914 is the most colossal breakdown in history of an economic system destroyed by its own inherent contradictions.

All the historical forces whose task it has been to guide the bourgeois society, to speak in its name and to exploit it, have declared their historical bankruptcy by the War. They defended capitalism as a system of human civilization, and the catastrophe born out of that system is primarily their catastrophe. The first wave of events raised the national governments and armies to unprecedented heights never attained before. For the moment the nations rallied around them. But the more terrible will be the crash of the governments when the people, deafened by the thunder of the cannon, realize the meaning of the events now taking place in all their truth and frightfulness.

The revolutionary reaction of the masses will be all the more powerful the more prodigious the cataclysm which history is now bringing upon them.

Capitalism has created the material conditions of a new Socialist economic system. Imperialism has led the capitalist nations into historic chaos. The War of 1914 shows the way out of this chaos by violently urging the proletariat on to the path of Revolution.

For the economically backward countries of Europe the War brings to the fore problems of a far earlier historic origin – problems of democracy and national unity. This is in a large measure the case with the peoples of Russia, Austria-Hungary, and the Balkan Peninsula. But these historically belated questions, which were bequeathed to the present epoch as a heritage from the past, do not alter the fundamental character of the events. It is not the national aspirations of the Serbs, Poles, Romanians or Finns that has mobilized twenty-five million soldiers and placed them in the battlefields, but the imperialistic interests of the bourgeoisie of the Great Powers. It is imperialism that has upset completely the European *status quo*, maintained for forty five years, and raised again the old questions which the bourgeois revolution proved itself powerless to solve. Yet in the present epoch it is quite impossible to treat these questions in and by themselves. They are utterly devoid of an independent character. The creation of normal relations of national life and economic development on the Balkan Peninsula is unthinkable if Czarism and Austria-Hungary are preserved. Czarism is now the indispensable military reservoir for the financial imperialism of France and the conservative colonial power of England. Austria-Hungary is the mainstay of Germany's imperialism. Issuing from the private family clashes between the national Serbian terrorists and the Hapsburg political police, the War very quickly revealed its true fundamental character – a struggle of life and death between Germany and England. While the simpletons and hypocrites prate of the defence of national freedom and independence, the German English War is really being waged for the freedom of the imperialistic exploitation of the peoples of India and Egypt on the one hand, and for the imperialistic division of the peoples of the earth on the other.

Germany began its capitalistic development on a national basis with the destruction of the continental hegemony of France in the year 1870-1871. Now that the development of Germany industry on a national foundation has transformed Germany into the first 'capitalistic power of the world, she finds herself colliding with the hegemony of England in her further course of development. The complete and unlimited domination of the European continent seems to Germany the indispensable prerequisite of the overthrow of her world enemy. The first thing, therefore, that imperialistic Germany writes in her program is the creation of a Middle European League of Nations. Germany, Austria-Hungary, the Balkan Peninsula and Turkey, Holland, the Scandinavian countries, Switzerland, Italy, and, if possible, enfeebled France and Spain and Portugal, are to make one economic and military whole, a Great Germany under the hegemony of the present German state.

This program, which has been thoroughly elaborated by the economists, political students, jurists and diplomats of German imperialism and translated into reality by its strategists, is the most striking proof and most eloquent expression of the fact that capitalism has expanded beyond the limits of the national state and feels intolerably cramped within its boundaries. The national Great Power must go and in its place must step the imperialistic World Power.

In these historical circumstances the working class, the proletariat, can have no interest in defending the outlived and antiquated national "fatherland", which has become the main obstacle to economic development. The task of the proletariat is to create a far more powerful fatherland, with far greater power of resistance – *the republican United States of Europe*[2] as the foundation of the United States of the World.

The only way in which the proletariat can meet the imperialistic perplexity of capitalism is by opposing to it as a practical program of the day the Socialist organization of world economy.

War is the method by which capitalism, at the climax of its development, seeks to solve its insoluble contradictions. To this. method the proletariat must oppose its own method, the method of the Social Revolution.

The Balkan question and the question of the overthrow of Czarism, propounded to us by the Europe of yesterday, can be solved only in a revolutionary way, in connection with the problem of the United Europe of tomorrow. The immediate, urgent task of the Russian Social Democracy, to which the author belongs, is the fight against Czarism. What Czarism primarily seeks in Austria-Hungary and the Balkans is a market for its political methods of plunder, robbery and acts of violence. The Russian bourgeoisie all the way up to its radical intellectuals has become completely demoralized by the tremendous growth of industry in the last five years, and it has entered into a bloody league with the dynasty, which had to secure to the impatient Russian capitalists their part of the world's booty by new land robberies. While Czarism stormed and devastated Galicia, and deprived it even of the rags and tatters of liberty granted to it by the Hapsburgs, while it dismembered unhappy Persia, and from the corner of the Bosphorus strove to throw the noose around the neck of the Balkan peoples, it left to the liberalism which it despised the task of concealing its robbery by sickening declamations over the defence of Belgium and France. The year 1914 spells the complete bankruptcy of Russian liberalism, and makes the Russian proletariat the sole champion of the war of liberation. It makes the Russian Revolution definitively an integral part of the Social Revolution of the European proletariat.

In our war against Czarism, in which we have never known a "national" truce[3] we have never looked for help from Hapsburg or Hohenzollern militarism, and we are not looking for it now. We have preserved a sufficiently clear revolutionary vision to know that the idea of destroying Czarism was utterly repugnant to German imperialism. Czarism has been its best ally on the Eastern border. It is united to it by close ties of social structure and historical aims. Yet even if it were otherwise, even if it could be assumed that, in. obedience to the logic of military operations, it would deal a destructive blow to Czarism, in defiance of the logic of its own political interests – even in such a highly improbable case we should refuse to regard the Hohenzollerns as an ally by sympathy or even by identity of immediate aims. The fate of the Russian Revolution is so inseparably bound up with the fate of European Socialism, and we Russian Socialists stand so firmly on the ground of internationalism, that we cannot, we must not for a moment, entertain the idea of purchasing the doubtful liberation of Russia by the certain destruction of the liberty of Belgium and France, and – what is more important still – thereby inoculating the German and Austrian proletariat with the virus of imperialism.

We are united by many ties to the German Social Democracy. We have all gone through the German Socialist school, and learned lessons from its successes as well as from its failures. The German Social Democracy was to us not only a party of the International ... It was the Party par excellence. We have always preserved and fortified the fraternal bond that united us with the Austrian Social Democracy. On the other hand we have always taken pride in the fact that we have made our modest contribution towards winning the franchise in Austria and arousing revolutionary tendencies in the German working class.[4] It cost more than one drop of blood to do it. We have unhesitatingly accepted moral and material support from our older brother who fought for the same ends as we on the other side of our Western border.

Yet it is just because of this respect for the past, and still more out of respect for the future, which ought to unite the working class. of Russia with the working classes of Germany and Austria, that we indignantly reject the "liberating" aid which German imperialism offers us in a Krupp munitions box, with the blessing, alas! of German Socialism. And we hope that the indignant protest of Russian Socialism will be loud enough to be heard in Berlin and in Vienna.

The collapse of the Second International[5] is a tragic fact, and it were blindness or cowardice to close one's eyes to it. The position taken by the French and by the larger part of English Socialism is as much a part of this breakdown as is the position of the German and Austrian Social Democracy. If the present work addresses itself chiefly to the German Social Democracy it is only because the German party was the strongest, most influential, and in principle the most basic member of the Socialist world. Its historic capitulation reveals most clearly the causes of the downfall of the Second International.

At first glance it may appear that the social revolutionary prospects of the future are wholly deceptive. The insolvency of the old Socialist parties has become catastrophically apparent. Why should we have faith in the future of the Socialist movement? Such scepticism, though natural, nevertheless leads to quite an erroneous conclusion. It leaves out of account the good will of history, just as we have often been too prone to ignore its ill will, which has now so cruelly shown itself in the fate that has overcome the International.

The present War signalizes the collapse of the national states. The Socialist parties of the epoch now concluded were national parties. They had become ingrained in the national states with all the different branches of their organizations, with all their activities and with their psychology. In the face of the solemn declarations at their congresses they rose to the defence of the conservative state, when imperialism, grown big on the national soil, began to demolish the antiquated national barriers. And in their historic crash the national states have pulled down with them the national Socialist parties also.

It is not Socialism that has gone down, but its temporary historical external form. The revolutionary idea begins its life anew as it casts off its rigid shell. This shell is made up of living human beings, of an entire generation of Socialists that has become fossilized in the self-abnegating work of agitation and organization through a period of several decades of political reaction, and has fallen into the habits and views of national opportunism or possibilism. All efforts to save the Second International on the old basis, by personal diplomatic methods and mutual concessions, are quite hopeless. The old mole of history is now digging its passageways all too well and none has the power to stop him.

As the national states have become a hindrance to the development of the forces of production, so the old Socialist parties have become the main hindrance to the revolutionary movement of the working class. It was necessary that they should demonstrate to the full their extreme backwardness, that they should discredit their utterly inadequate and narrow methods, and bring the shame and horror of national discord upon the proletariat, in order that working class might emancipate itself, through these fearful disillusionments, from the prejudices and slavish habits of the period of preparation, and become at last that which the voice of history is now calling it to be the revolutionary class fighting for power.

The Second International has not lived in vain. It has accomplished a huge cultural work. There has been nothing like it in history before. It has educated and assembled the oppressed classes The proletariat does not now need to begin at the beginning. It enters on the new road not with empty hands. The past epoch has bequeathed to it a rich arsenal of ideas. It has bequeathed to it the weapons of criticism. The new epoch will teach the proletariat to combine the old weapons of criticism with the new criticism of weapons.[6]

This book was written in extreme haste, under conditions far from favourable to systematic work. A large part of it is devoted to the old International which has fallen. But the entire book, from the first to the last page, was written with the idea of the New International constantly in mind, the New International which must rise up out of the present world cataclysm, the International of the last conflict and the final victory.

Leon Trotsky

Part I.

Chapter I.
The Balkan Question

"The War at present being waged against Russian Czarism and its vassals is dominated by a great historic idea. The impetus of this great historic idea consecrates the battlefields of Poland and of Eastern Russia. The roar of cannon, the rattling of machine guns, and the onrush of cavalry, all betoken the enforcement of the democratic program for the liberation of the nations. Had Czarism, in league with the French capitalistic powers and in league with an unscrupulous 'nation of shopkeepers',[7] not succeeded in suppressing the Revolution of 1905, the present slaughter of the nations would have been avoided.

"A democratic Russia would never have consented to wage this unscrupulous and futile War. The great ideas of freedom and justice now speak the persuasive language of the machine gun and the sword, and every heart susceptible of sympathy with justice and humanity can only wish that the power of Czarism may be destroyed once for all, and the oppressed Russian nationalities may again secure the right to decide their own destinies."

The above quotation is from the *Nepszava* of August 31, 1914, the official organ of the Socialist party of Hungary. Hungary is the land whose entire inner It [?] was erected upon the high handed oppression of the national minorities, upon the enslavement of the labouring classes, upon the official parasitism and usury of the ruling caste of large landowners. It is the land in which men like Tisza are masters of the situation, dyed-in-the-wool agrarians, with the manners of political bandits. In a word, Hungary is a country closest of kin to Czar ruled Russia.

So what is more fitting that that the Nepszava, the Socialist organ of Hungary, should hail with outbursts of enthusiasm the liberating mission of the German and Austro-Hungarian armies? Who other than Count Tisza could have felt the call to "enforce the democratic program for the liberation of the nations"? Who was there to uphold the eternal principles of law and justice in Europe but the ruling clique of Budapest, the discredited Panamists.[8] Would you entrust this mission to the unscrupulous diplomacy of "perfidious Albion"[9] to the nation of shopkeepers?

Laughter turns away wrath. The tragic inconsistencies of the policies followed by the International not only reach their climax in the articles of the poor Nepszava; they disarm us by their humour.

The present series of events began with the ultimatum sent to Serbia by Austria-Hungary. There was not the slightest reason why the international Social Democracy should take under its protection the intrigues of the Serbs or any other of the petty dynasties of the Balkan Peninsula. They were all endeavouring to hide their political adventures under the cloak of national aspirations. We had still less cause to lash ourselves into a state of moral indignation because a fanatic young Serb responded to the cowardly, criminal and wi national politics of the Vienna and Budapest government authorities with a bloody assassination. [It is noteworthy that these opportunistic Austrian and German Socialists are now writhing with moral indignation over the "treacherous assassination at Sarajavo". And yet they always sympathized with the Russian terrorists more than we, the Russian Social Democrats, did, who are opposed on principle to the terroristic method. Lost in the mist of chauvinism, they can no longer see that the unfortunate Serbian terrorist, Gavrilo Princip, represents precisely the same national principle as the German terrorist, Sand. Perhaps they will even as us to transfer our sympathies from Sand to Kotzebue? Or perhaps these eunuchs will advise the Swiss to overthrow the monuments erected to assassin Tell and replace them with monuments to the Austrian governor, Geissler, one of the spiritual forerunners of the murdered Archduke? – *L. T.*]

Of one thing we have no doubt. In the dealings between the Danube Monarchy and the Serbian government, the historic right, that is to say, the right of free development, rests entirely with Serbia, just as Italy was in the right in the year 1859. Underneath the dud between the imperial police scoundrels and the terrorists of Belgrade, there is hidden a far deeper meaning than merely the breed of the Karageorgevitches or the crimes of the Czar's diplomacy. On one side were the imperialistic claims of a national state that had lost its vitality, and on the other side, the striving of the dismembered Serbian nation to re-integrate itself into a national whole and become a living vital state.

Is it for this that we have sat so long in the school of Socialism to forget the first three letters of the democratic alphabet? This absolute lapse of memory, moreover, made its appearance only after the 4th of August. Up to that fatal date the German Marxists showed that they knew very well what was happening in South Eastern Europe.

On July 3, 1914, after the assassination at Sarajevo, the *Vorwärts* wrote:

"The bourgeois revolution of the South Slavs is in full swing, and the shooting at Sarajevo, however wild and senseless an act in itself is as much a chapter of this revolution as the battles by which the Bulgarians, Serbs, and Montenegrens liberated the peasants of Macedonia from the yoke of Turkish feudal exploitation. Is it a wonder that the South Slavs of Austria-Hungary look with longing to their racial brothers in the kingdom of Serbia? The Serbs in Serbia have attained the highest goal a people can attain in the present order of society. They have attained national independence. Whereas in Vienna or Budapest they treat every one bearing the name of Serb or Croatian with blows and kicks, with court-martial justice and the gallows ... There are seven and a half million South Slavs who, as a result of the victories in the Balkans, have grown bolder than ever in demanding their political rights. And if the imperial throne of Austria continues to resist their impact, it will topple over and the entire Empire with which we have coupled our destiny will break to pieces. For it is in line with historic evolution hat such national revolutions should march onward to victory."

If the International Social Democracy together with its Serbian contingent, offered its unyielding resistance to Serbia's national claims, it was certainly not out of any consideration for the historic rights of Austria-Hungary to oppress and disintegrate the nationalities living within her borders; and most certainly not out of consideration for the liberating mission of the Hapsburgs. Until August 1914[10] no one, except the black and yellow hirelings of the press, dared to breathe a word about that. The Socialists were influenced in their course of conduct by entirely different motives. First of all, the proletariat, although by no means disputing the historic right of Serbia to strive for national unity, could not trust the solution of this problem to the powers then controlling the destinies of the Serbian kingdom. And in the second place – and this was for us the deciding factor – the international Social Democracy could not sacrifice the peace of Europe to the national cause of the Serbs, recognizing, as it did, that, except for a European revolution, the only way such unity could be achieved was through a European war.

But from the moment Austria-Hungary carried the question of her own fate and that of Serbia to the battlefield, Socialists could no longer have the slightest doubt that social and national progress would be hit much harder in South Eastern Europe by a Hapsburg victory than by a Serbian victory. To be sure, there was still no reason for us Socialists to identify our cause with the aims of the Serbian army. This was the idea that animated the Serbian Socialists, Ljaptchevitch and Katzlerovitch, when they took the manly stand of voting against the war credits. [To appreciate fully this action of the Serbian Socialists we must bear in mind the political situation by which they were confronted. A group of Serbian conspirators had murdered a member of the Hapsburg family, the mainstay of Austro-Hungarian clericalism, militarism, and imperialism. Using this as a welcome pretext, the military parry in Vienna sent an ultimatum to Serbia, which for sheer audacity, has scarcely ever been paralleled in diplomatic history. In reply, the Serbian government made extra-ordinary concessions, and suggested that the solution of the question in dispute be turned over to the Hague tribunal. Thereupon Austria declared war on Serbia. If the idea of a "war of defence" has any meaning at all, it certainly applied to Serbia in this instance. Nevertheless, our friends, Ljaptchevitch and Katzlerovitch, unshaken in their conviction of the course of action that they as Socialists must pursue, refused the government a vote of confidence. The writer was in Serbia at the beginning of the War. In the Skuptchina, in an atmosphere of indescribable national enthusiasm. a vote was taken on the war credits. The voting was by roll-call. Two hundred members had answered "Yes". Then in a moment of deathlike silence came the voice of the Socialist Ljaptchevitch "No". Everyone felt the moral force of this protest, and the scene has remained indelibly impressed upon my memory. – *L. T.*] But surely we had still less reason to support the purely dynastic rights of the Hapsburgs and the imperialistic interests of the feudal-capitalistic cliques against the national struggle of the Serbs. At all events, the Austro-Hungarian Social Democracy, which now invokes its blessings upon the sword of the Hapsburgs for the liberation of the Poles, the Ukrainians, the Finns and the Russian people, must first of all clarify its ideas on the Serbian question, which has gotten so hopelessly muddled.

The question at issue, however, is not confined to the fate of the ten million Serbs. The clash of the European nations has brought up the entire Balkan question anew. The Peace of Bucharest[11] signed in 1903, has solved neither the national nor the international problems in the Near East. It has only intensified the added confusion resulting from the two unfinished Balkan Wars, unfinished because of the complete temporary exhaustion of the nations participating in it.

Romania had followed in the path of Austro-Hungarian politics, despite the Romanesque sympathies of its population, especially in the cities. This was due not so much to dynastic causes, to the fact that a Hohenzollern prince occupied the throne, as to the imminent danger of a Russian invasion. In 1879 the Russian Czar, as thanks for Romania's support in the Russo-Turkish War of "liberation", cut off a slice of Romanian territory, the province of Bessarabia. This eloquent deed provided a sufficient backing to the dynastic sympathies of the Hohenzollern in Bucharest. But the Magyar-Hapsburg clique succeeded in incensing the Romanian people against them by their denationalizing policy in Transylvania, which has a population of three million Romanians as against three-fourths of a million in the Russian province of Bessarabia; and they further antagonized them by their commercial treaties, which were dictated by the interests of the large Austro-Hungarian landowners. So that Romania's entrance into the War on the side of the Czar, despite the courageous and active agitation against participation in the War on either side, carried on by the Socialist party under the leadership of my friends Gherea and Rakovsky, is to be laid altogether at the door of the ruling class of Austria-Hungary, who are reaping the harvest they have sown here as well as elsewhere.

But the matter is not disposed of by fixing the historical responsibility. Tomorrow, in a month, in a year or more the War will bring to the foreground the whole question of the destiny of the Balkan peoples and of Austria-Hungary, and the proletariat will have to have its answer to this question. European democracy in the nineteenth century looked with distrust at the Balkan people's struggle for independence, because it feared that Russia might be strengthened at the expense of Turkey. On this subject Karl Marx wrote in 1853, on the eve of the Crimean War:

"It may be said that the more firmly established Serbia and the Serbian nationality is, the more the direct influence of Russia on the Turkish Slavs is shoved into the background. For in order to be able to maintain its position as a state, Serbia had to import its political institutions, its schools ... from Western Europe."

This prophesy has been brilliantly fulfilled in what has actually happened in Bulgaria, which was created by Russia as an outpost on the Balkans. As soon as Bulgaria was fairly well established as a national state, it developed a strong anti-Russian party, under the leadership of Russia's former pupil, Stambulov, and this party was able to stamp its iron seal upon the entire foreign policy of the young country. The whole mechanism of the political parties in Bulgaria is so constructed as to enable it to steer between the two European combinations without being absolutely forced into the channel of either, unless it chooses to enter it of its own accord. Romania went with the Austro-German alliance, Serbia, since 1903, with Russia, because the one was menaced directly by Russia, the other by Austria. The more independent the countries of South East Europe are front Austria-Hungary, the more effectively they will be able to protect their independence against Czarism.

The balance of power in the Balkans, created by the Congress of Berlin[12] in 1879, was full of contradictions. Cut up by artificial ethnographical boundaries, placed under the control of imported dynasties from German nurseries, bound hand and foot by the intrigues of the Great Powers, the peoples of the Balkans could not cease their efforts for further national freedom and unity. The national politics of independent Bulgaria was naturally directed towards Macedonia, populated by Bulgarians. The Berlin Congress had left it under Turkish rule. On the other hand, Serbia had practically nothing to look for in Turkey with the exception of Sanjak, Novy Bazar. Its national interests lay on the other side of the Austro-Hungarian boundary, in Bosnia-Herzegovina, Croatia, Slovenia and Dalmatia. Romania had no interests in the South, where it is separated from European Turkey by Serbia and Bulgaria. Romania's expansion policy was directed towards the North West and the East, towards Hungarian Transylvania and Russian Bessarabia. Finally, the national expansion of Greece, like that of Bulgaria, collided with Turkey. Austro-German politics, aiming at the artificial preservation of European Turkey, broke down not on account of the diplomatic intrigues of Russia, although these of course were not lacking. It broke down because of the inevitable course of evolution. The Balkan Peninsula had entered on the path of capitalist development, and it was this fact that raised the question of the self-determination of the Balkan peoples as national states to the historical issue of the day.

The Balkan War disposed of European Turkey, and thereby created the conditions necessary for the solution of the Bulgarian and Greek questions. But Serbia and Romania, whose national completion could only be achieved at the expense of Austria-Hungary, found themselves checked in their efforts at expansion southwards, and were compensated at the expense of what racially belonged to Bulgaria – Serbia in Macedonia, and Romania in Dobrudja. This is the meaning of the second Balkan War and the Peace of Bucharest by which it was concluded. The mere existence of Austria-Hungary, this Turkey of Middle Europe, blocks the way to the natural self-determination of the peoples of the South-East. It compels them to keep constantly fighting against each other, to seek support against each other from the outside, and so makes them a tool of the political combinations of the Great Powers. It was only in such chaos that Czarist diplomacy was enabled to spin the web of its Balkan politics, the last thread of which was Constantinople. And only a federation of the Balkan states, both economic and military, can interpose an invincible barrier to the greed of Czarism.

Now that European Turkey has been disposed of, it is Austria-Hungary that stands in the way of a federation of the Balkan states. Romania, Bulgaria, and Serbia would have found their natural boundaries, and would have united with Greece and Turkey, on the basis of common economic interests, into a league of defence. This would finally have brought peace to the Balkan Peninsula, that witches' cauldron which periodically threatened Europe with explosions, until it drew it into the present catastrophe. Up to a certain time the Socialists had to reconcile themselves to the routine way in which the Balkan question was treated by capitalistic diplomats, who in their conferences and secret agreements stopped up one hole only to open another, even wider one. So long as this dilatory method kept postponing the final solution, the Socialist International could hope that the settlement of the Hapsburg succession would be a matter not for a European war, but for the European Revolution. But now that the War has destroyed the equilibrium of the whole of Europe, and the predatory Powers are seeking to remodel the map of Europe – not on the basis of national democratic principles, but of military strength – the Social Democracy must come to a clear comprehension of the fact that one of the chief obstacles to freedom, peace and progress, in addition to Czarism and German militarism, is the Hapsburg Monarchy as a state organization.

The crime of the Galician Socialist group under Daszynski consisted not only in placing the Polish cause above the cause of Socialism, but also linking the fate of Poland with the fate of the Austro-Hungarian armies and the fate of the Hapsburg Monarchy. The Socialist proletariat of Europe cannot adopt such a solution of the question. For us the question of united and independent Poland is on a par with the question of united and independent Serbia. We cannot and we will not permit the Polish question to be solved by methods which will perpetuate the chaos at present prevailing in South-Eastern Europe, in fact through the whole of Europe. For us Socialists the independence of Poland means its independence on both fronts, on the Romanov front and on the Hapsburg front. We not only wish the Polish people to be free from the oppression of Czarism. We wish also that the fate of the Serbian people shall not be dependent upon the Polish nobility in Galicia.

For the present we need not consider what the relations of an independent Poland will be to Bohemia, Hungary and the Balkan. Federation. But it is perfectly clear that a complex of medium sized and small states on the Danube and in the Balkan Peninsula will constitute a far more effective bar to the Czarist designs on Europe than the weak, chaotic Austro-Hungarian State, which proves its right to existence only by its continued attempts upon the peace of Europe.

In the article of 1853, quoted above, Marx wrote as follows on the Eastern question:

"We have seen that the statesmen of Europe, in their obdurate stupidity, petrified routine, and hereditary intellectual indolence, recoil from every attempt at answering the question of what is to become of Turkey in Europe. The driving force that favours Russia's; advance towards Constantinople is the very means by which it is thought to keep her away from it, the empty theory, never carried out, of maintaining the *status quo*. What is this *status quo*? For the Christian subjects of the Porte[13] it means nothing else than the perpetuation of their oppression by Turkey. As long as they are under the yoke of the Turkish rule, they look upon the head of the Greek Church, the ruler of 60 million Greek Church Christians, as *their natural protector and liberator*."

What is here said of Turkey now applies in a still greater degree to Austria-Hungary. The solution of the Balkan question is unthinkable without the solution of the Austro-Hungarian question, as they are both comprised in one and the same formula – the Democratic Federation of the Danube and Balkan Nations.

"The governments with their old-fashioned diplomacy," wrote Marx, "will never solve the difficulty. Like the solution of so many other problems, the Turkish problem, too, is reserved for the European Revolution." This statement holds just as good today as when it was first written. But for the Revolution to solve the difficulties that have piled up in the course of centuries, the proletariat must have its own program for the solution of the Austro-Hungarian question. And this program it must oppose just as strenuously to the Czaristic greed of conquest as to the cowardly and conservative efforts to maintain the Austro-Hungarian *status quo*.

Chapter II.
Austria-Hungary

Russian Czarism undoubtedly represents a cruder and more barbarian form of state organisation than does the feebler absolutism of Austria-Hungary, which has been mitigated by the weakness of old age. But Russian Czarism and the Russian state are by no means identical. The destruction of Czarism does not mean the disintegration of the state. On the contrary it means its liberation and its strengthening. All such assertions, as that it is necessary to push Russia back into Asia, which found an echo even in certain Social Democratic organs, are based on a poor knowledge of geography and ethnography. Whatever may be the fate of various parts of present Russia – Russian Poland, Finland, the Ukraine or Bessarabia – European Russia will not cease to exist as the national territory of a many-millioned race that has made notable conquests along the line of cultural development during the last quarter century.

Quite different is the case of Austria-Hungary. As a state organization it is identical with the Hapsburg Monarchy. It stands or falls with the Hapsburgs, just as European Turkey was identical with the feudal-military Ottoman caste and fell when that caste fell.[14] A conglomerate of racial fragments centrifugal in tendency, yet forced by a dynasty to stick together, Austria-Hungary presents the most reactionary picture in the very heart of Europe. Its continuation after the present European catastrophe would not only delay the development of the Danube and Balkan peoples for more decades to come and make a repetition of the present War a practical certainty, but it would also strengthen Czarism politically by preserving its main source of spiritual nourishment.

If the German Social Democracy reconciles itself to the ruin of France by regarding it as punishment for France's alliance with Czarism, then we must ask that the same criterion be applied to the German-Austrian alliance. And if the alliance of the two Western democracies with a despotic Czarism gives the lie to the French and English press when they represent the war as one of liberation, then is it not equally arrogant, if not more so, for the German Social Democracy to spread the banner of liberty over the Hohenzollern army, the army that is fighting not only *against* Czarism and its allies , but also *for* the entrenchment of the Hapsburg Monarchy?

Austria-Hungary is indispensable to Germany, to the ruling class in Germany as we know it. When the ruling Junker class[15] threw France into the arms of Czarism by the forceful annexation of Alsace-Lorraine[16] and systematically embittered the relations with England by rapidly increasing naval armaments; when it repulsed all attempts at an understanding with the Western democracies because such an understanding would have implied the democratization of Germany, then this ruling class saw itself compelled to seek support from the Austro-Hungarian Monarchy as a reserve source of military strength against the enemies in the East and the West.

According to the German point of view the mission of the Dual Monarchy[17] was to place Hungarian, Polish, Romanian, Czech, Ruthenian, Serbian and Italian auxiliaries in the service of the German military and Junker policy. The ruling class in Germany had easily reconciled itself to the expatriation of ten to twelve millions Germans, for these twelve millions formed the kernel around which the Hapsburgs united a non-German population of more than forty million. A democratic federation of independent Danube nations would have made these peoples useless as allies of German militarism. Only a monarchy in Austria-Hungary, a monarchy enforced by militarism, would make that country of any value as an ally to Junker Germany. The indispensable condition for this alliance, sanctified by the Nibelungen troth[18] of dynasties, was the military preparedness of Austria-Hungary, a condition to be achieved in no other way than by the mechanical suppression of the centrifugal national tendencies.

Since Austria-Hungary is surrounded on all sides by states composed of the same races as are within its borders, its foreign policy is necessarily intimately connected with its internal policy. To keep seven million Serbs and South Slavs within the frame of its own military state, Austria-Hungary is compelled to extinguish the hearth-fire that kindles their political leanings – the independent kingdom of Serbia.

Austria's ultimatum to Serbia was the decisive step in this direction. took this step under the pressure of necessity," wrote Eduard Bernstein in *Die Sozialistisehe Monatshefte* (No.16). To be sure it did, if political events are considered from the viewpoint of dynastic necessity.

To defend the Hapsburg policy on the ground of the low moral standard of the Belgrade rulers is to close one's eyes to the fact that the Hapsburgs did make friends with Serbia, but only when Serbia was under the most despicable government that the history of the unfortunate Balkan Peninsula has known, that is, when it had at its head an Austrian agent, Milan. The reckoning with Serbia came as late because the efforts made at self-preservation were too weak in the enfeebled organism of the Dual Monarchy. But after the death of the Archduke, the support and hope of the Austrian military party – and of Berlin – Austria's ally gave her. a sharp dig in the ribs, insisting upon a demonstration of firmness and strength. Not only was Austria's ultimatum to Serbia approved of in advance by the rulers of Germany, but, according to all information, it was actually inspired from that quarter. The evidence is plainly set forth in the very same *White Book* which professional and amateur diplomats offer as a document of the Hohenzollern love of peace.

After defining the aims of Greater Serbian propaganda and the machinations of Czarism in the Balkans, the *White Book* states:

"Under such conditions Austria was forced to the realization that it was not compatible with the dignity or the self-preservation of the Monarchy to look on at the doings across the border and remain passive. The Imperial Government informed us of this view and asked for our opinion. We could sincerely tell our ally that we agreed with his estimate of the situation and could assure him that any action he might find necessary to put an end to the movement in Serbia against the Austrian Monarchy would meet with our approval. In doing so, we were well aware of the fact that eventual war operations on the part of Austria-Hungary might bring Russia into the field and might, according to the terms of our alliance, involve us in a war.

"But in view of the vital interests of Austria-Hungary that were at stake, we could not advise our ally to show a leniency incompatible with his dignity, or refuse him our support in a moment of such grave portent. We were the less able to do so because our own interests also were vitally threatened by the persistent agitation in Serbia. If the Serbs, aided by Russia and France, had been allowed to go on endangering the stability of our neighbouring Monarchy, this would have led to the gradual breakdown of Austria and to the subjection of all the Slavic races to the Russian rule. At this in turn would have made the position of the Germanic race in Central Europe quite precarious. An Austria morally weakened, breaking down before the advance of Russian Pan-Slavism, would not be an ally with whom we could reckon and on whom we could depend, as we are obliged to depend, in the face of the increasingly threatening attitude of our neighbours to the East and the West. We therefore left Austria a free hand in its action against Serbia."

The relation of the ruling class in Germany to the Austro-Serbian conflict is here fully and clearly defined. it is not merely that Germany was informed by the Austrian Government of the latter's intentions, not merely that she approved them, and not merely that she accepted the consequences of fidelity to an ally. No, Germany looked on Austria's aggression as unavoidable, as a saving act for herself, and actually made it *a condition of the continuance of the alliance*. Otherwise, "Austria would not be an ally with whom we could reckon."

The German Marxists were fully aware of this state of affairs and of the dangers lurking in it. On June 29th, a day after the murder of the Austrian Archduke, the *Vorwärts* wrote as follows:

"The fate of our nation has been all too closely knit with that of Austria as a result of a bungling foreign policy. Our rulers have made the alliance with Austria the basis of our entire foreign policy. Yet it becomes clearer every day that this alliance is a source of weakness rather than of strength. The *problem of Austria* threatens more and more to become *a menace to the peace of Europe*."

A month later, when the menace was about to culminate in the dread actuality of war, on July 28th, the chief organ of the German Social Democracy wrote in equally definite terms. "How shall the German proletariat act in the face of such a senseless paroxysm?" it asked; and then gave the answer: "*The German proletariat is not in the least interested in the preservation of the Austrian national chaos*."

Quite the contrary. Democratic Germany is far more interested in the disruption than in the preservation of Austria-Hungary. A disrupted Austria-Hungary would mean a gain to Germany of an educated population of twelve million and a capital city of the first rank, Vienna. Italy would achieve national completion, and would cease to play the role of the incalculable factor that she always has been in the Triple Alliance. An independent Poland, Hungary, Bohemia, and a Balkan Federation including a Romania of ten million inhabitants on the Russian frontier, would be a mighty bulwark against Czarism. And most important of all, a democratic Germany with a population of 75,000,000 Germans could easily, without the Hohenzollerns and the ruling Junkers, come to an agreement with France and England and could isolate Czarism and condemn its foreign and internal policies to complete impotence. A policy directed towards this goal would indeed be a policy of liberation for the people of Russia as well as of Austria-Hungary. But such a policy requires an essential preliminary condition, namely, that the German people, instead of entrusting the Hohenzollerns with the liberation of other nations, should set about liberating themselves from the Hohenzollerns.

The attitude of the German and Austro-Hungarian Social Democracy in this war is in blatant contradiction to such aims. At the present moment it seems convinced of the necessity of preserving and strengthening the Hapsburg Monarchy in the interests of Germany or of the German nation. And it is absolutely from this anti-democratic viewpoint – which drives the blush of shame to the cheek of every internationally minded Socialist that the *Wiener Arbeiter-Zeitung* formulates the historical meaning of the present War, when it declares "it is primarily a war (of the Allies) against the German spirit".

"Whether diplomacy has acted wisely, whether this has had to come, time alone can decide. Now the fate of the German nation is at stake! And there can be no hesitation, no wavering! The German people are one in the inflexible iron determination not to bend to the yoke, and neither death nor devil can succeed and so forth and so on. (*Wiener Arbeiter-Zeitung*, August 5th). We will not offend the political and literary taste of the reader by continuing this quotation. Nothing is said here about the mission of liberating other nations. Here the object of the war is to preserve and secure "German humanity".

The defence of *German* culture, *German* soil, *German* humanity seems to be the mission not only of the German army but of the Austro-Hungarian army as well. Serb must fight against Serb, Pole against Pole, Ukrainian against Ukrainian, for the sake of "German humanity". The forty million non-German nationalities of Austria-Hungary are considered as simply historical manure for the field of German culture. That this is not the standpoint of international Socialism, it is not necessary to point out. It is not even pure national democracy in its most elementary form. The Austro-Hungarian General Staff explains this "humanity" in its communique of September 18th: "All peoples of our revered monarchy, as our military oath says, 'against any enemy no matter whom', must stand together as one, vying with one another in courage."

The *Wiener Arbeiter-Zeitung* accepts in its entirety this Hapsburg-Hohenzollern viewpoint of the Austro-Hungarian problem as a non-national military reservoir. It is the same attitude as the militarists of France have toward the Senegalese and the Moroccans, and the English have toward the Hindus. And when we consider that such opinions are not a new phenomenon among the German Socialists of Austria, we have found the main reason why the Austrian Social Democracy broke up so miserably into national groups, and thus reduced its political importance to a minimum.

The disintegration of the Austrian Social Democracy into national parts fighting among themselves, is one expression of the inadequacy of Austria as a state organization. At the same time the attitude of the German-Austrian Social Democracy proved that it was itself the sorry victim of this inadequacy, to which it capitulated spiritually. When it proved itself impotent to unite the many-raced Austrian proletariat under the principles of Internationalism, and finally gave up this task altogether, the Austro-German Social Democracy subordinated all Austria-Hungary and even its own policies to the "Idea" of Prussian Junker Nationalism. This utter denial of principles speaks to us in an unprecedented manner from the pages of the *Wiener Arbeiter-Zeitung*. But if we listen more carefully to the tones of this hysterical nationalism we cannot fail to hear a graver voice, the voice of history telling us that the path of political progress for Central and South-Eastern Europe leads over the ruins of the Austro-Hungarian Monarchy.

Chapter III.
The War against Czarism

But how about Czarism? Would not Germany's and Austria's victory mean the defeat of Czarism? And would not the beneficent results of the defeat of Czarism greatly outbalance the beneficent results of a dismembered Austria-Hungary?

The German and Austrian Social Democrats lay much stress upon this question in the arguing they do about the War. The crushing of a small neutral country, the ruin of France – all this is justified by the need to fight Czarism. Haase gives as the reason for voting the war credits the necessity of "defence against the danger of Russian despotism". Bernstein goes back to Marx and Engels and quotes old texts for his slogan, "Settling with Russia!"

Sudekum dissatisfied with the result of his Italian mission, says that what the Italians are to blame for is not understanding Czarism. And when the Social Democrats of Vienna and Budapest fall in line under the Hapsburg banner in its "holy war" against the Serbians struggling for their national unity, they sacrifice their Socialistic honour to the necessity for fighting Czarism.

And the Social Democrats are not alone in this. The entire bourgeois German press has no other aims, for the moment, than the annihilation of the Russian autocracy, which oppresses the peoples of Russia and menaces the freedom of Europe.

The imperial Chancellor denounces France and England as vassals of Russian despotism. Even the German Major-General von Morgen, assuredly a true and tried "friend of liberty and independence", calls on the Poles to rebel against the despotism of the Czar.

But for us who have gone through the school of historical materialism it would be a disgrace if we did not perceive the actual relations of the interests in spite of these phrases, these lines, this boasting, this foul vulgarity and stupidity.

No one can genuinely believe that the German reactionaries really do cherish such a hatred of Czarism, and are aiming their blows against it. On the contrary, after the War Czarism will be the same to the rulers of Germany that it was before the War – the most closely related form of government. Czarism is indispensable to the Germany of the Hohenzollerns, for two reasons. In the first place, it weakens Russia economically, culturally and militaristically, and so prevents its development as an imperialistic rival. In the second place, the existence of Czarism strengthens the Hohenzollern Monarchy and the Junker oligarchy, since if there were no Czarism, German absolutism would face Europe as the last mainstay of feudal barbarism.

German absolutism never has concealed the interest of blood relationship that it has in the maintenance of Czarism, which represents the same social form though in more shameless ways. Interests, tradition, sympathies draw the German reactionary element to the side of Czarism. "Russia's sorrow is Germany's sorrow". At the same time the Hohenzollerns, behind the back of Czarism, can make a show of being the bulwark of culture "against barbarism", and can succeed in fooling their own people if not the rest of Western Europe.

"With sincere sorrow I see a friendship broken that Germany has kept faithfully," said Wilhelm II in his speech upon the declaration of war, referring neither to France nor to England, but to Russia, or rather, to the Russian dynasty, in accordance with the Hohenzollern's Russian religion, as Marx would have said.

We are told that Germany's political plan is to create, on the one hand, a basis of rapprochement with France and England by a victory over those countries, and, on the other hand, to utilize a strategic victory over France in order to crush Russian despotism.

The German Social Democrats must either have inspired Wilhelm and his chancellor with this plan, or else must have ascribed this plan to Wilhelm and his chancellor.

As a matter of fact, however, the political plans of the German reactionaries are of exactly the opposite character, must necessarily be of the opposite character.

For the present we will leave open the question of whether the destructive blow at France was dictated by strategic considerations, and whether "strategy" sanctioned defensive tactics on the Western front. But one thing is certain, that not to see that the policy of the Junkers required the ruin of France, is to prove that one has a reason for keeping one's eyes closed. France – France is the enemy!

Eduard Bernstein, who is sincerely trying to justify the political stand taken by the German Social Democracy, draws the following conclusions: Were Germany under a democratic rule, there would be no doubt as to how to settle accounts with Czarism. A democratic Germany would conduct a revolutionary war on the East. It would call on the nations oppressed by Russia to resist the tyrant and would give them the means wherewith to wage a powerful fight for freedom. (Quite right!). However, Germany is not a democracy, and therefore it would be a utopian dream (Exactly!) to expect any such policy with all its consequences from Germany as she is. (*Vorwärts*, August 28th.) Very well then! But right here Bernstein suddenly breaks off his analysis of the actual German policy "with all its consequences". After showing up the blatant contradiction in the position of the German Social Democracy, he closes with the unexpected hope that a reactionary Germany may accomplish what none hut a revolutionary Germany could accomplish. *Credo quia absurdum.*[19]

Nevertheless, it might be said in opposition to this that while the ruling class in Germany has naturally no interest in fighting Czarism, still Russia is now Germany's enemy, and, quite independently of the will of the Hohenzollerns, the victory of Germany over Russia might result in the great weakening, if not the complete overthrow of Czarism. Long live Hindenburg, the great unconscious instrument of the Russian Revolution, we might cry along with the *Chemnitz Volksstimme*. Long live the Prussian Crown Prince, also a quite unconscious instrument. Long live the Sultan of Turkey who is now serving in the cause of the Revolution by bombarding the Russian cities around the Black Sea. Happy Russian Revolution how quickly the ranks of her army are growing!

However, let us see if there is not something really to be said on this side of the question. Is it not possible that the defeat of Czarism might actually aid the cause of the Revolution?

As to such a *possibility*, there is nothing to be said against it. The Mikado and his Samurai were not in the least interested in freeing Russia, yet the Russo-Japanese War gave a powerful impetus to the revolutionary events that followed.[20]

Consequently similar results may be expected from the German-Russian War. But to place the right political estimate upon these historical possibilities we must take the following circumstances into consideration.

Those who believe that the Russo-Japanese War brought on the Revolution neither know nor understand historical events and their relations. The war merely hastened the outbreak of the Revolution; but for that very reason it also weakened it. For had the Revolution developed as a result of the organic growth of inner forces, it would have come later, but would have been far stronger and more systematic. Therefore, revolution has no real interest in war. This is the first consideration. And the second thing is, that while the Russo-Japanese War weakened Czarism, it strengthened Japanese militarism. The same considerations apply in a still higher degree to the present German-Russian War.

In the course of 1912-1914 Russia's enormous industrial development once and for all pulled the country out of its state of counter-revolutionary depression.[21]

The growth of the revolutionary movement on the foundation of the economic and political condition of the labouring masses, the growth of opposition in broad strata of the population, led to a new period of storm and stress. But in contrast to the years 1902-1905, this movement developed in a far more conscious, systematic manner, and, what is more, was based on a far broader social foundation. It needed time to mature, but it did not need the lances of the Prussian Samurai. On the contrary, the Prussian Samurai gave the Czar the opportunity of playing the role of defender of the Serbs, the Belgians and the French.

If we presuppose a catastrophic Russian defeat, the war may bring a quicker outbreak of the Revolution, but at the cost of its inner weakness. And if the Revolution should even gain the upper hand under such circumstances, then the bayonets of the Hohenzollern armies would be turned on the Revolution. Such a prospect cart hardly fail to paralyse Russia's revolutionary forces; for it is impossible to deny the lct tha the party of the German proletariat stands behind the Hohenzollern bayonets. But this is only one side of the question. The defeat of Russia necessarily presupposes decisive victories by Germany and Austria on the other battlefields, and this would mean the enforced preservation of the national-political chaos in Central and South-Eastern Europe and the unlimited mastery of German militarism in all Europe.

An enforced disarmament for France, billions in indemnities, enforced tariff walls around the conquered nations, and an enforced commercial treaty with Russia, all this in conjunction would make German imperialism master of the situation for many decades.

Germany's new policy, which began with the capitulation of the party of the proletariat to nationalistic militarism, would be strengthened for years to come. The German working class would feed itself, materially and spiritually, on the crumbs from the table of victorious imperialism, while the cause of the Social Revolution would have received a mortal blow.

That in such circumstances a Russian revolution, even if temporarily successful, would be an historical miscarriage, needs no further proof.

Consequently, this present battling of the nations under the yoke of militarism laid upon them by the capitalist classes contains within itself monstrous contrasts which neither the War itself nor the governments directing it can solve in any way to the interest of future historical development. The Social Democrats could not, and can not now, combine their aims with any of the historical possibilities of this War, that is, with either the victory of the Triple Alliance or the victory of the Entente.[22]

The German Social Democracy was once well aware of this. The *Vorwärts* in its issue of July 28th, discussing the very question of the war against Czarism, said:

"But if it is not possible to localize the trouble, if Russia should step into the field? What should our attitude toward Czarism be then? Herein lies the great difficulty of the situation. Has not the moment come to strike a death blow at Czarism? If German troops cross the Russian frontier, will that not mean the victory of the Russian Revolution?"

And the *Vorwärts* comes to the following conclusion:

"Are we so sure that it *will* mean victory to the Russian Revolution if German troops cross the Russian frontier? It may readily bring the collapse of Czarism, but will not the German armies fight a revolutionary Russia with even greater energy, with a keener desire for victory, than they do the absolutistic Russia?"

More than this. On August 3rd, on the eve of the historical session of the Reichstag, the *Vorwärts* wrote in an article entitled *The War Upon Czarism*:

"While the conservative press is accusing the strongest party in the Empire of high treason, to the rejoicing of other countries, there are other elements endeavouring to prove to the Social Democracy that the impending war is really an old Social Democratic demand. War against Russia, war upon the blood-stained and faithless Czarism – this last is a recent phrase of the press which once kissed the knout – isn't this what Social Democracy has been asking for from the beginning?

"These are literally the arguments used by one portion of the bourgeois press, in fact the more intelligent portion, and it only goes show what importance is attached to the opinion of that part of the German people which stands behind the Social Democracy The slogan no longer is 'Russia's sorrow is Germany's sorrow. Now it is 'Down with Czarism!' But since the days when the leaders of the Social Democracy referred to (Bebel, Lassalle, Engels, Marx) demanded a democratic war against Russia, Russia has quite ceased to be the mere palladium of reaction. Russia is also the seat of revolution. The overthrow of Czarism is now the task of all the Russian people, especially the Russian proletariat, and it is just the last weeks that have shown how vigorously this very working class in Russia is attacking the task that history has laid upon it ... And all the nationalistic attempts of the 'True Russians' to turn the hatred of the masses away from Czarism and arouse a reactionary hatred against foreign countries, particularly Germany, have failed so far. The Russian proletariat knows too well that its enemy is not beyond the border but within its own land. Nothing was more distasteful to these nationalistic agitators, the True Russians and Pan-Slavists, than the news of the great peace demonstration of the German Social Democracy. Oh, how they would have rejoiced had the contrary been the case, had they been able to say to the Russian proletariat, 'There, you see, the German Social Democrats stand at the head of those who are inciting the war against Russia.' And the Little Father[23] in St. Petersburg would also have breathed a sigh of relief and said, 'That is the news I wanted to hear. Now the backbone of my most dangerous enemy, the Russian Revolution is broken. The international solidarity of the proletariat is torn. Now I cart unchain the beast of nationalism. I am saved!'"

Thus wrote the *Vorwärts* after Germany had already declared war on Russia.

These words characterize the honest manly stand of the proletariat against a belligerent jingoism. The *Vorwärts* clearly understood and cleverly stigmatized the base hypocrisy of the knout-loving ruling class of Germany, which suddenly became conscious of its mission to free Russia from Czarism. The *Vorwärts* warned the German working class of the political extortion that the bourgeois press would practise on their revolutionary conscience. "Do not believe these friends of the knout," the *Vorwärts* said to the German proletariat. "They are hungry for your souls, and hide their imperialistic designs behind liberal-sounding phrases. They are deceiving you you, the cannon-fodder with souls that they need. If they succeed in winning you over, they will only be helping Czarism by dealing the Russian Revolution a fearful moral blow. And, if in spite of this, the Russian Revolution should raise its head, these very people will help Czarism to crush it."

That is the sense of what the *Vorwärts* preached to the working class up to the 4th of August.

And exactly three weeks later the same *Vorwärts* wrote: "Liberation from Muscovitism (?) freedom and independence for Poland and Finland, free development for the great Russian people themselves, dissolution of the unnatural alliance between the two cultural nations and Czarist barbarism - these were the aims that inspired the German people and made them ready for any sacrifice", and inspired also the German Social Democracy and its chief organ.

What happened in those three weeks to cause the *Vorwärts* to repudiate its original standpoint?

What happened? Nothing of importance. The German armies strangled neutral Belgium, burned down a number of Belgian towns, destroyed Louvain[24] the inhabitants of which had been so criminally audacious as to fire at the armed invaders when they themselves wore no helmets and were waving feathers. ["How characteristically Prussian,' wrote Marx to Engels, "to declare that no man may defend his 'fatherland' except in uniform!" – *L. T.*]

In those three weeks the German armies carried death and destruction into French territory, and the troops of their ally, Austria-Hungary, pounded the love of the Hapsburg Monarchy into the Serbs on the Save and the Drina. These are facts that apparently convinced the *Vorwärts* that the Hohenzollerns were waging the war of liberation of the nations.

Neutral Belgium was crushed, and the Social Democrats remained silent. And Richard Fischer was sent to Switzerland as special envoy of the Party to explain to the people of a neutral country that the violation of Belgian neutrality and the ruin of a small nation were a perfectly natural phenomenon. Why so much excitement? Any other European government, in Germany's place, would have acted in the same way. It was just at this time that the German Social Democracy not only reconciled itself to the War as a work of real or supposed national defence, but even surrounded the Hohenzollern-Hapsburg armies with the halo of an offensive campaign for freedom. What an unprecedented fall for a party that for fifty years had taught the German working class to look upon the German Government as the foe of liberty and democracy!

In the meantime every day of the War discloses the danger to Europe that the Marxists should have foreseen at once. The chief blows of the German Government were not aimed at the East, but at the West, at Belgium, France and England. Even if we accept the improbable premise that nothing but strategic necessity determined this plan of campaign, the logical political outcome of this strategy remains with all its consequences, that is, the necessity for a full and definite defeat of Belgium, France and the English land forces, so that Germany's hands might be free to deal with Russia.

Wasn't it perfectly clear that what was at first represented as a temporary measure of strategic necessity in order to soothe the German Social Democracy, would become an end in itself through the force of events? The more stubborn the resistance made by France, whose duty it has actually become to defend its territory and its independence against the German attack, the more certainly will the German armies be held on the Western front; and the more exhausted Germany is on the Western front, the less strength and inclination will remain for her supposedly main task, the task with which the Social Democracy credited her, the "settling with Russia". And then history will witness an "honourable" peace between the two most reactionary powers of Europe, between Nicholas, to whom fate granted cheap victories over the Hapsburg Monarchy "[Russian diplomacy is interested only in such wars," wrote Engels in 1890, "as force her allies to bear the chief burden of raising troops and suffering invasion, and leave to the Russian troops only the work of reserves. Czarism makes war on its own account only on decidedly weaker nations, such as Sweden, Turkey and Persia." – *L. T.*], Austria-Hungary must now be placed in the same class as Turkey and Persia, rotten to its core, and Wilhelm, who had his "settling", but with Belgium, not with Russia.

The alliance between Hohenzollern and Romanov – after the exhaustion and degradation of the Western nations – will mean a period of the darkest reaction in Europe and the whole world.

The German Social Democracy by its present policy smooths the way for this awful danger. And the danger will become an actuality unless the European proletariat interferes and enters as a revolutionary factor into the plans of the dynasties and the capitalist governments.

Notes For Part I

1. *Revolutions and wars* refers to the French Revolutionary Wars after 1789, the wars for the unification of Germany and Italy, the Franco-Prussian war of 1870, and finally the Paris Commune of 1871.
2. This slogan was used by the Russian Social Democrats in 1914 and 1915 and was later withdrawn for tactical reasons.
3. The concept of "national truce" (*Burgfriede*) was based on an old medieval custom that private quarrels should cease when the castle was besieged.
4. The Revolution of 1905 in Russia shook Czarism to its foundations and forced the autocracy to made temporary concessions, conceding some democratic rights. The Revolution also had a profound international impact.
5. The German Social Democratic deputies voted for war credits on August 4th 1914, a date marking the collapse of the Second International.
6. The phrase is from Marx's *Introduction to a Contribution to the Critique of Hegel's Philosophy of Right* (1844).
7. A reference to Britain.
8. The Panama Canal Company collapsed in February 1889. The scandal reached many prominent people.
9. A reference to England.
10. See note 5. Austria actually declared war on Serbia on July 28th 1914.

11. The first Balkan War began in October 1912 and the final war ended in 1914. The Turkish Ottoman Empire was forced to give up all its European territory. The state of Albania was created by the Treaty of London 1913. The Second Balkan War ended with the Treaty of Bucharest in July 1913.
12. At the Congress of Berlin in 1878 the Great Powers carved up the states of South Eastern Europe.
13. A reference to the Court of the Ottoman Empire in Constantinople.
14. Trotsky's prediction of the disintegration of the Austro-Hungarian Empire proved correct.
15. Ultra-conservative Prussian landlords with large estates in the East of the country.
16. A disputed region between France and Germany.
17. The Dual monarchy was established in a compromise between the Austrian government and the Hungarian opposition in 1867. Collapsed at the end of the world war.
18. From the German classical poem *Nibelungenlied*, a troth between hero and betrayer.
19. (Latin) I believe that which is absurd.
20. Russia was defeated by Japan in 1904, on land and at sea, in a battle for control of Manchuria and Korea. The discontent over the defeat contributed to the outbreak of the 1905 Revolution.
21. Counter-revolutionary depression refers to the situation in Russia after the victory of the reaction following the defeat of the 1905 revolution.
22. The Triple Alliance was initially of Germany, Austria and Italy, but Italy broke away in 1906. The Entente was the military alliance of France, Britain and Russia.
23. Little Father is Czar Nicholas II.
24. Louvain or Leuven, is an old university town in Belgium. Destroyed in the opening weeks of the war by the German attack.

Glossary Of Names

August Bebel (1840-1913). Marxist of working class origin, co-founder with Wilhelm Leibknecht of German Social Democracy in 1869. Leader of the German SD and the 2nd International in pre-war years.

Eduard Bernstein (1850-1932). German Social Democrat. Lived in exile for decades. Leading proponent of revisionist and reformist ideas in the 2nd International. Took a centrist position during WW1.

Otto von Bismarck (1815-1898). Dominated the German and European political scene 1862-1890 as Chancellor. Unified Germany under the domination of Prussia and the Hohenzollerns.

Bonaparte, Louis, (1808-1873). Nephew of Napoleon Bonaparte, Emperor of France 1852-1870.

Ignacy Daszynski (1866-1936). Leader of the Galician Polish Socialists. Anti-Russian chauvinist.

Constantin Dobrogeanu-Gherea, (1855-1920). Romanian Marxist. Founder and Leader of Romanian Social Democracy.

Richard Fischer (1855-1926). German Social Democrat, Party Secretary from 1899. Right wing, supported the war. From 1902 manager of *Vorwärts*,the Party paper. Expelled (anti-war) members from staff of Vorwärts.

Hugo Haase (1863-1919). German Social Democrat. Succeeded Bebel as leader of SD Parliamentary fraction 1913. Opposed voting for war credits within the Party but succumbed to Majority decision. Founder and leader of Independent Social Democratic Party (USPD) 1916. Shot on the steps of the Reichstag by a Monarchist officer.

Hapsburg Dynasty. Originating in the 13th Century, from 1867 the Hapsburg family ruled over the Austro-Hungarian empire until 1918.

Paul von Hindenberg (1847-1934). Prussian militarist. Fought in war against France 1870-71. General in 1903. Retired 1911. Recalled at beginning of War. Victor at Tannenburg 1914 and the Masurian Lakes 1915 against Russia. Later Field Marshal. Succeeded Ebert as President 1925. Co-existed with Hitler from 1932 till his death.

Hohenzollern Dynasty. Emerged as rulers of Prussia in 17th Century. From 1870 the family ruled a unified Germany. Overthrown in 1918 on the abdication of Kaiser Wilhelm II.

Karageorgevitch. The ruling family of Serbia, founded by Karageorge Petrovich who led the 1st Balkan uprising against the Ottoman Empire in 1804. Peter Karageorge took power in Belgrade by coup d'etat in 1903.

Trishcha Katzlerovitch (1879-??). Founder of Serbian Social Democracy. In Serbian parliament from 1908-1921. Anti-militarist. Attended Kienthal Conference. Founder and Chairman Serbian Communist Party, and when this was banned, formed the Independent Labour Party.

Alfred Krupp (1812-1887). German industrialist, steel tycoon and munitions manufacturer. In 1871, at the founding of the German Empire, was the leader of German industry. Son, Frederick Alfred Krupp (1854-1902), was a personal friend of the Kaiser.

Ferdinand Lassalle (1825-1864). German socialist. Founder of the General Association of German Workers (1863). Very influential figure in German workers' movement. His followers later helped form the German Social Democracy.

Karl Leibknecht (1871-1919). Left Wing German Social Democrat. Member German Reichstag and Prussian Landtag. Anti-militarist. Drafted during the war, he was imprisoned for anti-war activity, May 1916 to November 1918. Leader Spartacus League. One of the leaders of the Berlin uprising 1919. Assassinated by counter-revolutionary soldiers, January 15th 1919, with Rosa Luxemburg

Wilhelm Leibnecht (1826-1900). Friend of Marx, founder and leader of the German Social Democracy. Reichstag Deputy. Jailed 1872 for opposition to the Franco-Prussian War.

Rosa Luxemburg (1870-1919). Polish Socialist. Joined German Social Democracy 1897. With Karl Liebknecht led Left Wing. Imprisoned many times for anti-war activity. Leader of the Spartacist League and founder of the German Communist Party. Assassinated by reactionary officers January 15th, 1919.

Helmuth von Moltke, (The Younger) (1848-1916). Nephew of the Elder Moltke. German Chief of Staff in the early years of World War I.

von Morgan, Major General. German Division Commander on the Russian Front.

Obrenovich. Alternative ruling family of Serbia (to the Karageorges). Dynasty founded by Milos (1780-1860) who ruled 1830-39 and 1858-1860. Son, Milan ruled 1868-89. Grandson Alexander (1876-1903), the last of the dynasty, was assassinated with his wife 1903.

Gavrilo Princip (1895-1918). Revolutionary Serb nationalist from Bosnia. Shot Archduke Franz Ferdinand and his wife on 28 June 1914 at Sarajevo precipitating WW1. Sentenced to life imprisonment, died in prison.

Christian Georgievich Rakovsky (1873-1941?). Bulgarian by birth. Member Romanian Social Democracy since the 1890s. Imprisoned 1916 for anti-war activity. Released by Russian troops 1917, went to Russia and joined the Communists. Held various Government and diplomatic posts. Victim of Stalinist purges.

Romanovs. Ruling dynasty of Russia 1613-1917.

Karl Ludwig Sand. Jena theology student who was executed for the assassination of Kotzebue in 1819.

Stefan Nokolov Stambulov (1854-1895). Bulgarian statesman. Figured in rising of 1875-6 against Great Powers, Chief of Russophile regency 1886. Premier 1887-1894. Forced to retire. Assassinated.

Albert Oskar Wilhelm Sudekum (1871-1944). German Right-Wing Social Democrat. Revisionist and chauvinist. Visited Italy and Romania in attempt to win over Socialists to German Imperialism.

Istvan Tisza (1861-1918). Hungarian Premier 1903-5 and 1913-1917. Pro-German.

Wilhelm I (1797-1888). King of Prussia 1861-1871 and German Emperor 1871-1888.

Wilhelm II (1859-1941). German Emperor 1888-1918. Last Hohenzollern ruler. Overthrown by the November 1918 revolution, retired to Holland.

The War and the International
Part II.

Chapter IV.
The War against the West

ON his return from his diplomatic trip to Italy, Dr. Südekum wrote in the *Vorwaerts* that the Italian comrades did not sufficiently comprehend the nature of Czarism. We agree with Dr. Südekum that a German can more easily understand the nature of Czarism as he experiences daily, in his own person, the nature of Prussian-German absolutism. The two "natures" are very closely akin to each other.

German absolutism represents a feudal-monarchical organization, resting upon a mighty capitalist foundation, which the development of the last half-century has erected for it. The strength of the German army, as we have learned to know it anew in its present bloody work, consists not alone in the great material and technical resources of the nation, and in the intelligence and precision of the workman-soldier, who had been drilled in the school of industry and his own class organizations. It has its foundations also in its Junker officer caste, with its master class traditions, its oppression of those who are below and its subordination to those who are above. The German army, like the German state, is a feudal-monarchical organization with inexhaustible capitalist resources. The bourgeois scribblers may chatter all they want about the supremacy of the German, the man of duty, over the Frenchman, the man of pleasure; the real difference lies not in the racial qualities, but in the social and political conditions. The standing army, that closed corporation, that self-sufficing state within the state, remains, despite universal military service, a caste organization that in order to thrive must have artificial distinctions of rank and a monarchical top to crown the commanding hierarchy.

In his work, *The New Army*, Jaurès showed that the only army France could have is one of defence built on the plan of arming every citizen, that is, a democratic army, a militia. The bourgeois French Republic is now paying the penalty for having made her army a counterpoise to her democratic state organization. She created, in Jaurès' words, "a bastard regime in which antiquated forms clashed with newly developing forms and neutralized each other." This incongruity between the standing army and the republican regime is the fundamental weakness of the French military system.

The reverse is true of Germany. Germany's barbarian retrograde political system gives her a great military supremacy. The German bourgeoisie may grumble now and then when the praetorian caste spirit of the officers' corps leads to outbreaks like that of Zabern.[25] They may make wry faces at the crown Prince and his slogan, "Give it to them! Give it to them!" The German Social Democracy may inveigh ever so sharply against the systematic personal ill-treatment of the German soldier, which has caused proportionately twice as many suicides in the German barracks as in the barracks of any other country. But for all that, the fact that the German bourgeoisie has absolutely no political character and that the German Socialist party has failed to inspire the proletariat with the revolutionary spirit has enabled the ruling class to erect the gigantic structure of militarism, and so place the efficient and intelligent German workmen under the command of the Zabern heroes and their slogan, "Give it to them".

Professor Hans Delbrück seeks the source of Germany's military strength in the ancient model of Teutoburgerwald,[26] and he is perfectly justified.

"The oldest Germanic system of warfare," he writes, "was based on the retinue of princes, a body of specially selected warriors, and the mass of fighters comprising the entire nation. This is the system we have today also. How vastly different are the methods of fighting now from those of our ancestors in the Teutoburgerwald! We have the technical marvels of modern machine guns. We have the wonderful organization of immense masses of troops, and yet our military system is at bottom the same. The martial spirit is raised to its highest power, developed to its utmost in a body which once was small but now numbers many thousands, a body giving fealty to their War Lord, and by him, as by the princes of old, regarded as his comrades; and under their leadership the whole people, educated by them and disciplined by them. *Here we have the secret of the warlike character of the German nation.*"

The French Major, Driant, looks on at the German Kaiser in his white cuirassier's uniform, undoubtedly the most imposing military uniform in the world, and republican by constraint that he is, his heart is filled with a lover's jealousy. And how the Kaiser spends his time "in the midst of his army, that true family of the Hohenzollerns!" The Major is fascinated.

The feudal caste, whose hour of political and moral decay had struck long ago, found its connection with the nation once more in the fertile soil of imperialism. And this connection with the nation has taken such deep root that the prophecies of Major

Driant, written several years ago, have actually come true prophecies that until now could only have appeared as either the poisonous promptings of a secret Bonapartist, or the drivelling of a lunatic.

"The Kaiser," he wrote is the Commander in Chief and behind him stands the entire working class of Germany as one man ... Bebel's Social Democrats are in the ranks, their fingers on the trigger, and they too think only of the welfare of the Fatherland. The ten-billion war indemnity that France will have to pay will be a greater help to them than the Socialist chimeras on which they fed the day before."

Yes, and now they are writing of this future indemnity even in some *Social Democratic* (!) papers, with open rowdy insolence 'an indemnity, however, not of ten billions, but of twenty or thirty billions.

Germany's victory over France – a deplorable strategic necessity, according to the German Social Democrats – would mean not only the defeat of France's standing army; it would mean primarily the victory of the feudal-monarchical state over the democratic-republican state.

For the ancient race of Hindenburgs, Moltkes and Klucks, hereditary specialists in mass-murder, are just as indispensable a condition of German victory as are the 42 centimetre guns, the last word in human technical skill.

The entire capitalist press is already talking of the unshakable stability of the German Monarchy, strengthened by the War. And German professors, the same who proclaimed Hindenburg a doctor of All the Sciences, are already declaring that political slavery is a higher form of social life.

"The democratic republics, and the so-called monarchies that are under subjection to a parliamentary regime, and all the other beautiful things that were so extolled 'what little capacity they have shown to resist the storm!"

These are the things that the German professors are writing now. It is shameful and humiliating enough to read the expressions of the French Socialists, who had proved themselves too weak to break the alliance of France with Russia or even to prevent the return to three years' military service, but who, when the War began, never the less donned their red trousers and set out to free Germany. But we are seized with a feeling of unspeakable indignation on reading the German Socialist party press, which in the language of exalted slaves extols the brave heroic caste of hereditary oppressors for their armed exploits on French territory.

On August 15, 1870, when the victorious German armies were approaching Paris, Engels wrote in a letter to Marx, after describing the confused condition of the French defence: "Nevertheless, a revolutionary government, if it comes soon, need not despair. But it must leave Paris to its fate, and continued carry on the war from the South. It is then still possible that such a government may hold out until arms and ammunition are brought and a new army organized with which the enemy can be gradually pushed back to the frontier. That would be the right ending to the war for both countries to demonstrate that they cannot be conquered."

And yet there are people who shout like drunken helots, "On to Paris." And in doing so they have the impudence to invoke the names of Marx and Engels. In what measure are they superior to the thrice despised Russian liberals who crawled on their bellies before his Excellency, the military Commander, who introduced the Russian knout into East Galicia. It is cowardly arrogance this talk of the purely "strategic" character of the war on the Western front. Who takes any account of it? Certainly not the German ruling classes. They speak the language of conviction and of main force. They call things by their right names. They know what they want and they know how to fight for it.

The Social Democrats tell us that the War is being waged for the cause of national independence. "That is not true," retorted Herr Arthur Dix.

"Just as the high politics of the last century," wrote Dix, "owed its specially marked character to the *National Idea*, so the political- world events of this century stand under the emblem of the *Imperialistic Idea*. The imperialistic idea that is destined to give the impetus, the scope and the goal to the striving for power of the great." (*Der Weltwirtschaftskrieg*, 1914, p.3).

"It shows gratifying sagacity," says the same Herr Arthur Dix, "on the part of those who had charge of the military preparations of the war, that the advance of our armies against France and Russia in the very first stage of the War took place precisely where it was most important to keep valuable German mineral wealth free from foreign invasion, and to occupy such portions of the enemy's territory as would supplement our own underground resources" (*Ibid.*, p.38)

The "strategy" of these wait and see Socialists, who now speak in whispers, really begins with the robbery of mineral wealth. The Social Democrats tell us that the War is a war of defence.

But Herr George Irmer says clearly and distinctly:

"People ought not to be talking as through it were a settled thing that the German nation had come too late for rivalry for world economy and world dominion 'that the world has already been divided. Has not the earth been divided over and over again in all epochs of history?" (*Los vom englischen Weltjoch*, 1914, p.42.)

The Socialists try to comfort us by telling us that Belgium has only been temporarily crushed and that the Germany will soon vacate their Belgian quarters. But Herr Arthur Dix, who knows very well what he wants, and who has the right and the power to want it, writes that what England fears most, and expressly so, is that *Germany should have an outlet to the Atlantic Ocean.*

"For this very reason, he continues, "we must *neither let Belgium go out of our hands*, nor must we fail to make sure that the coast line from Ostend to the Somme shall not again fall into the hands of any state which may become a political vassal of England. We must see to it that in some form or other *German influence is securely established there*."

In the endless battles between Ostend and Dunkirk, sacred "strategy" is now carrying out this program of the Berlin stock exchange, also.

The Socialists tell us that the War between France and Germany is merely a brief prelude to a lasting alliance between those countries. But here, too, Herr Arthur Dix shows all the cards. According to him, "there is but one answer: *to seek to destroy the English world' s trade, and to deal deadly blows at English national economy*."

"The aim for the foreign policy of the German Empire for the next decades is clearly indicated," Professor Franz von Liszt announces. "Protection against England,' that must be our slogan." (*Ein mitteleuropaischer Staatenverband*, 1914, p.24.)

"We must crush the most treacherous and malicious of our foes, cries a third. "We must break the tyranny which England exercises over the sea with base self-seeking and shameless contempt of justice and right."

The War is directed not against Czarism, but primarily against England's supremacy on the sea.

"It may be said," Professor Schiemann confesses, "that no success of ours has given us such joy as the defeat of the English at Maubeuge and St. Quentin on August 28th."

The German Social Democrats tell us that the chief object of the War is the 'settlement with Russia". But plain, straightforward Herr Rudolf Theuden wants to give Galicia to Russia with North Persia thrown in. Then Russia "would have got enough to be satisfied for many decades to come. We may even make her our friend by it."

"What ought the War to bring us?" asks Theuden, and then he answers:

"*The chief payment must be made us by France....* France must give us Belfort, that part of Lorraine which borders on the Moselle, and, in case of stubborn resistance, that part as well which borders the Maas. If we make the Maas and the Moselle German boundaries, the French will some day perhaps wean themselves away from the idea of making the Rhine a French boundary."

The bourgeois politicians and professors tell us that England is the chief enemy; that Belgium and France are the gateway to the Atlantic Ocean; that the hope of a Russian indemnity is only a Utopian dream, anyway; that Russia would be more useful as friend than as foe; that France will have to pay in land and in gold – and the *Vorwaerts* exhorts the German workers to "hold out until the decisive victory is ours."

And yet the *Vorwaerts* tells us that the War is being waged for the independence of the German nation, and for the liberation of the Russian people. What does this mean? Of course we must look for ideas, logic and truth where they do not exist. This is simply a case of an ulcer of slavish sentiments bursting open and foul pus crawling over the pages of the working men's press. It is clear that the oppressed class which proceeds too slowly and inertly on its way toward freedom must in the final hour drag all its hopes and promises through mire and blood, before there arises in its soul the pure, unimpeachable voice - 'the voice of revolutionary honour.

Chapter V.
The War of defence

"THE thing for us to do now is to avert this danger (Russian' despotism), and to secure the culture and independence of our land. Thus we will make good our word, and do what we have always said we would. In the hour of danger we will not leave our Fatherland in the lurch ... Guided by these principles we vote for the war credits."

This was the declaration of the German Social Democratic fraction, read by Haase in the Reichstag session of August 4th. Here only the defence of the fatherland is mentioned. Not a word is said of the "liberating" mission of this War in behalf of the peoples of Russia, which was later sung in every key by the Social Democratic press. The logic of the Socialist press, however, did not keep pace with its patriotism. For while it made desperate efforts to represent the War as one of pure defence, to secure the safety of Germany's possessions, it at the same time pictured it as a revolutionary offensive war for the liberation of Russia and of Europe from Czarism.

We have already shown clearly enough why the peoples of Russia had every reason to decline with thanks the assistance offered them at the point of the Hohenzollern bayonets. But how about the "defensive" character of the War?

What surprises us even more than what is said in the declaration of the Social Democracy is what it conceals and leaves unsaid. After Hollweg had already announced in the Reichstag the accomplished violation of the neutrality of Belgium and Luxembourg as a means of attacking France, Haase does not mention this fact in a single word. This silence is so monstrous that one is tempted to read the declaration a second and a third time. But in vain. The declaration is written as though such countries as Belgium, France and England had never existed on the political map of the German Social Democracy.

But facts do not cease to be facts simply because political parties shut their eyes to them. And every member of the International has the right to ask this question of

Comrade Haase, "What portion of the five billions voted by the Social Democratic fraction was meant for the destruction of Belgium?" It is quite possible that in order to protect the German fatherland from Russian despotism it was inevitable that the Belgian fatherland should be crushed. But why did the Social Democratic fraction keep silent on this point?

The reason is clear. The English Liberal government, in its effort to make the War popular with the masses, made its plea exclusively on the ground of the necessity of protecting the independence of Belgium and the integrity of France, but utterly ignored its alliance with Russian Czarism. In like manner, and from the same motives, the German Social Democracy speaks to the masses only about the war against Czarism, but does not mention even by name Belgium, France and England. All this is of course not exactly flattering to the international reputation of Czarism. Yet it is quite distressing that the German Social Democracy should sacrifice its own good name to the call to arms against Czarism. Lassalle said that every great political action should begin with a statement of things as they are. Then why does the defence of the fatherland begin with an abashed silence as to things as they are? Or did the German Social Democracy perhaps think that this was not a "big political action"?

Anyway, the defence of the fatherland is a very broad and very elastic conception. The world catastrophe began with Austria's ultimatum to Serbia. Austria, naturally, was guided solely by the need of defending her borders from her uneasy neighbour. Austria's prop was Germany. And Germany, in turn, as we already know, was prompted by the need to secure her own state. "It would be senseless to believe," writes Ludwig Quessel on this point, "that one wall could be torn away from this extremely complex structure (Europe) without endangering the security of the whole edifice."

Germany opened her "defensive war with an attack upon Belgium, the violation of Belgium's neutrality being allegedly only a means of breaking through to France along the line of least resistance. The military defeat of France also was to appear only as a strategic episode in the defence of the fatherland.

To some German patriots this construction of things did not seem quite plausible, and they had good grounds for disbelieving it. They suspected a motive which squared far better with the reality. Russia, entenag upon a new era of military preparation, would be a far greater menace to Germany in two or three years than she was then. And France during that time would have completely carried out her three year army reform. Is it not clear, then, that an intelligent self-defence demanded that Germany should not wait for the attack of her enemies but should anticipate them by two years and take the offensive at once? And isn't it clear, too, that such an offensive war, deliberately provoked by Germany and Austria, is in reality a preventive war of defence?

Not infrequently these two points of view are combined in a single argument. Granted that there is some slight contradiction between them. The one declares that Germany did not want the War now and that it was forced upon her by the Triple Entente, while the other implies that war was disadvantageous to the Entente now and that for that very reason Germany had taken the initiative to bring on the War at this time. But what if there is this contradiction? It is lightly and easily glossed over and reconciled in the saving concept of a war of defence.

But the belligerents on the other side disputed this advantageous position of being on the defensive, which Germany sought to assume, and did it successfully. France could not permit the defeat of Russia on the ground of her own self-defence. England gave as the motive for her interference the immediate danger to the British Islands which a strengthening of Germany's position at the mouth of the Channel would mean. Finally, Russia, too, spoke only of self-defence. It is true that no one threatened Russian territory. But national possessions, mark you, do not consist merely in territory, but in other, intangible factors as well, among them, the influence over weaker states. Serbia "belongs" in the sphere of Russian influence and serves the purpose of maintaining the so-called balance of power in the Balkans, not only the balance of power among the Balkan States but also between Russian and Austrian influence. A successful Austrian attack on Serbia threatened to disturb this balance of power in Austria's favour, and therefore meant an indirect attack upon Russia. Sasonov undoubtedly found his strongest argument in Quessel's words: "It would be senseless to believe that one wall could be torn away from the extremely complex structure (Europe) without endangering the security of the entire edifice."

It is superfluous to add that Serbia and Montenegro, Belgium and Luxembourg, could also produce some proofs of the defensive character of their policy. Thus, all the countries were on the defensive, none was the aggressor. But if that is so, then what sense is there in opposing the claims of defensive and offensive war to each other? The standards applied in such cases differ greatly, and are not frequently quite incommensurable.

What is of fundamental importance to us Socialists is the question of the historical role of the War. Is the War calculated to effectively promote the productive forces and the state organizations, and to accelerate the concentration of the working class forces Or is the reverse true, will it act as a hindrance? This materialistic evaluation of wars stands above all formal or external considerations, and in its nature has no relation to the question of defence or aggression. And yet sometimes these formal expressions about a war designate with more or less truth the actual significance of the war. When Engels said that the Germans were on the defensive in 1870, he had least of all the immediate political and diplomatic circumstances in mind. The determining fact for him was that in that war Germany was fighting for her right to national unity, which was a necessary condition for the economic development of the country and the Socialist consolidation of the proletariat. In the same sense the Christian peoples of the Balkans waged a war of defence against Turkey, fighting for their right to independent national development against the foreign rule.

The question of the immediate international political conditions leading to a war is independent of the value the war possesses from the *historico-materialistic* point of view. The German war against the Bonapartist Monarchy was historically unavoidable. In that war the right of development was on the German side. Yet those historical tendencies did not, in themselves, predetermine the question as to which party was interested in provoking the war just in the year 1870. We know now very well that international politics and military considerations induced Bismark to take the actual initiative in the war. It might have happened just the other way, however. With greater foresight and energy, the government of Napoleon III could have anticipated Bismarck, and begun the war a few years earlier. That would have radically changed the immediate political aspect of the events, but it would have made no difference in the historic estimate of the war.

Third in order is the factor of diplomacy. Diplomacy here has a twofold task to perform. First, it must bring about war at the moment most favourable for its own country from the international as well as the military standpoint. Second, it must employ methods which throw the burden of responsibility for the bloody conflict, in public opinion, on the enemy government. The exposure of diplomatic trickery, cheating and knavery is one of the most important functions of Socialist political agitation. But no matter to what extent we succeed in this at the crucial juncture, it is clear that the net of diplomatic intrigues in themselves signifies nothing either as regards the historic role of the war or its real initiators. Bismarck's clever manoeuvres forced Napoleon III to declare war on Prussia although the actual initiative came from the German side.[27]

Next follows the purely military aspect. The *strategic* plan operations can be calculated chiefly for defence or attack, regardless of which side declared the war and under what conditions. Finally, the first tactics followed in the carrying out of the plan not infrequently play a great part in a strategic estimating the war as a war of defence or of aggression.

"It is a good thing," wrote Engels to Marx on July 31, 1870, "that the French attacked first on German soil. If the Germans repel the invasion and follow it up by invading French territory then it will certainly not produce the same impression as if the Germans had marched into France without a previous invasion In this way the war remains, on the French side, more Bonapartistic.

Thus we see by the classic example of the Franco Prussian War that the standards for judging whether a war is defensive or aggressive are full of contradictions when two nations clash. Then how much more so are they when it is a clash of several nations. If we unroll the tangle from the beginning, we arrive at the following connection between the elements of attack and defence. The first tactical move of the French should, at least in Engels' opinion, make the people feel that the responsibility of attack rested with the French. And yet the entire *strategic* plan of the Germans had an absolutely aggressive character. The *diplomatic* moves of Bismarck forced Bonaparte to declare war against his will and thus appear as the disturber of the peace of Europe, while the military-political initiative in the war came from the Prussian government. These circumstances are by no means of slight importance for the *historical* estimate of the war, but they are not at all exhaustive.

One of the causes of this war was the growing ambition of the Germans for national self-determination which conflicted with the dynastic pretensions of the French Monarchy. But this national "war of defence" led to the annexation of Alsace-Lorraine and so in its second stage turned into a dynastic war of conquest.

The correspondence between Marx and Engels shows that they were guided chiefly by historical considerations in their attitude towards the war of 1870. To them, of course, it was by no meaps a matter of indifference as to who conducted the war and flow it conducted. "Who would have thought it possible," Marx writes bitterly, "that twenty-two years after 1848 a nationalist war in Germany could have been given such theoretical expression." Yet what was of decisive significance to Marx and Engels was the objective consequences of the war. "If the Prussians triumph, it will mean the centralization of the state power – useful to the centralization of the German working class."

Liebknecht and Bebel, starting with the same historical estimate of the war, were directly forced to take a political position toward it. It was by no means in opposition to the views of Marx and Engels, but, on the contrary, with their perfect acquiescence that Liebknecht and Bebel refused, in the Reichstag, to take any responsibility for this war. The statement they handed in read:

"We cannot grant the war appropriations that the Reichstag is asked to make because that would be a vote of confidence in the Prussian government ... As opponents on principle of every dynastic war, as Social Republicans and members of the International Labour Association, which, without distinction of nationality fights all oppressors and endeavours to unite all the oppressed in one great brotherhood, we cannot declare ourselves either directly or indirectly in favour of the present war."

Schweitzer acted differently. He took the historical estimate of the war as a direct guide for his tactics – one of the most dangerous of fallacies! – and in voting the war credits gave a vote of confidence to the policy of Bismarck. And this in spite of the fact that it was necessary, if the centralization of state power arising out of the War was to prove useful to the Social Democratic cause, that the working class should from the very beginning oppose the dynastic-Junker centralization with their own class-centralization filled with revolutionary distrust of the rulers.

Schweitzer's political attitude invalidated those very consequences of the War which had induced him to give a vote of confidence to the makers of the War.

Forty years later, drawing up the balance sheet of his life-work, Bebel wrote:

"The attitude that Liebknecht and I took at the outbreak and during the continuance of the war has for years been a subject of discussion and violent attack, at first even in the Party; but only for a short time. Then they acknowledged that we had been right. I confess that I do not in any way regret our attitude, and if at the outbreak of the war we had known what we learned within the next few years from the official and unofficial disclosures, our attitude from the very start would have been still harsher. We would not merely have abstained, as we did, from voting the first war credits, we would have voted *against* them." (*Autobiography*, Part II, p.167.)

If we compare the Liebknecht-Bebel statement of 1870 with Haase's declaration in 1914, we must conclude that Bebel was mistaken when he said, "Then they acknowledged that we had been right." For the vote of August 4th was eminently a condemnation of Bebel's policy forty-four years earlier, since in Haase's phraseology, Bebel had then left the fatherland in the lurch in the hour of danger. What political causes and considerations have led the party of the German proletariat to abandon its glorious traditions? Not a single weighty reason has been given so far. All the arguments adduced are full of contradictions. They are like diplomatic communiques which are written to justify an already accomplished act. The leader writer of *Die Neue Zeit* writes – with the blessing of Comrade Kautsky; that Germany's position towards Czarism is the same as it was towards Bonapartism in 1870. He even quotes from a letter of Engels: "All classes of the German people realized that it was a question, first of all, of national existence, and so they fell in line at once." For the same reason, we are told, the German Social Democracy has fallen in line now. It is a question of national existence. "Substitute Czarism for Bonapartism, and Engels' words are true today." And yet the fact remains, in all its force, that Bebel and Liebknecht demonstratively refused to vote either money or confidence to the government in 1870. Does it not hold just as well, then, if we "substitute Czarism for Bonapartism"? To this question no answer has been vouchsafed.

But what did Engels really write in his letter concerning the tactics of the labour party?

"It does not seem possible to me that under such circumstances a German political party can preach *total obstruction*, and place all sorts of minor considerations above the main issue." *Total obstruction!* – But there is a wide gap between total obstruction and the total capitulation of a political party. And it was this gap that divided the positions between Bebel and Schweitzer in 1870. Marx and Engels were with Bebel against Schweitzer. Comrade Kautsky might have informed his leader writer, Hermann Wendel, of this fact. And it is nothing but defamation of the dead for *Simplicissimus* now to reconcile the shades of Bebel and Bismarck in Heaven. If *Simplicissimus* and Wendel have the right to awaken anybody from his sleep in the grave for the endorsement of the present tactics of the German Social Democracy then it is not Bebel, but Schweitzer. It is the shade of Schweitzer that now oppresses the political party of the German proletariat.

But the very analogy between the Franco-Prussian War and the present War is superficial and misleading in the extreme. Let us set aside all the international relations. Let us forget that the War meant first of all the destruction of Belgium, and that Germany's main force was hurled not against Czarism but republican France. Let us forget that the starting point of the War was the crushing of Serbia, and that one of its aims was the strengthening and consolidation of the arch-reactionary state, Austria-Hungary. We will not dwell on the fact that the attitude of the German Social Democracy dealt a hard blow at the Russian Revolution, which in the two years before the War had again flared up in such a tempest. We will close our eyes to all these facts, just as the German Social Democracy did on August 4th, when it did not see that there was a Belgium in the world, a France, England, Serbia, or Austria-Hungary. We will grant only the existence of Germany.

In 1870, it was quite easy to estimate the historical significance of the war. "If the Prussians win, the centralization of state power will further the centralization of the German working class." And now?

What would be the result for the German working class of a Prussian victory now? The only territorial expansion which the German working class could welcome, because it would complete the national unity, is a union of German Austria with Germany. Any other expansion of the German fatherland means another step towards the transformation of Germany from a national state to a state of nationalities, and the consequent introduction of all those conditions which render more difficult the class struggle of the proletariat.

Ludwig Frank hoped – and he expressed this hope in the language of a belated Lassallean – that later, after a victorious war, he would devote himself to the work of the "internal building up" of the state. There is no doubt that Germany will need this "internal building up" after a victory no less than before the War. But will a victory make this work easier? There is nothing in Germany's historical experiences any more than in those of any other country to justify such a hope.

"We regarded the doings of the rulers of Germany (after the victories of 1870) as a matter of course," says Bebel in his *Autobiography*. "It was merely an illusion of the Party Executive to believe that a more liberal spirit would prevail in the new order. And this more liberal regime was to be granted by the same man who had till then shown himself the greatest enemy, I will not say of democratic development, but even of every liberal tendency, and who now as victor planted the heel of his cuirassier boot on the neck of the new Empire." (Vol.II, p.188)

There is absolutely no reason to expect different results now from a victory from above. On the contrary. In 1870 Prussian Junkerdom had first to adapt itself to the new imperial order. It could not feel secure in the saddle all at once. It was eight years after the victory over France before the anti-Socialist laws[28] were passed. In these forty-four years Prussian Junkerdom has become the imperial Junkerdom. And if, after half a century of the most intense class struggle, Junkerdom should appear at the head of the victorious nation, then we need not doubt that it would not have felt the need of Ludwig Frank's services for the internal building up of the state had he returned safe from the fields of German victories. But far more important than the strengthening of the class position of the rulers is the influence a German victory would have upon the proletariat itself. The War grew out of imperialistic antagonisms between the capitalist states, and the victory of Germany, as stated above, can produce only one result territorial acquisitions at the expense of Belgium, France and Russia, commercial treaties forced upon her enemies, and new colonies. The class struggle of the proletariat would then be placed upon the basis of the imperialistic hegemony of Germany, the working class would be interested in the maintenance and development of this hegemony, and revolutionary Socialism would for a long time be condemned to the role of a propagandist sect.

Marx was right when in 1870 he foresaw, as a result of the German victories, a rapid development for the German labour movement under the banner of scientific Socialism. But now the international conditions point to the very opposite prognosis. Germany's victory would mean taking the edge off the revolutionary movement, its theoretic shallowing, and the dying out of the Marxist ideas.

Chapter VI.
What have Socialists to do with Capitalist Wars?

But the German Social Democracy, we shall be told does not want victory. Our answer must be in the first place that this is not true. What the German Social Democracy wants is told by its press. With two or three exceptions Socialist papers daily point out to the German workingman that a victory of the German arms is his victory. The capture of Maubeuge, the sinking of three English warships, or the fall of Antwerp aroused in the Social Democratic press the same feelings that otherwise are excited by the gain of a new election district or a victory in a wage dispute. We must not lose sight of the fact that the German labour press, the Party press as well as the trade union papers, is now a powerful mechanism that in place of the education of the people's will for the class struggle has substituted the education of the people's will for military victories. I have not in mind the ugly chauvinistic excesses of individual organs, but the underlying sentiment of the overwhelming majority of the Social Democratic papers. The signal for this attitude seems to have been given by the vote of the fraction on August 4th.

But the fraction was not thinking of a German victory. It made it its task only to avert the danger threatening from the outside, to defend the fatherland. That was all. And here we come back to the question of wars of defence and wars of aggression. The German press, including the Social Democratic organs, does not cease to repeat that it is Germany of all countries that finds itself on the defensive in this War. We have already discussed the standards for determining the difference between a war of aggression and a war of defence. These standards are numerous and contradictory. Yet in the present case they testify unanimously that Germany's military acts cannot possibly he construed as the acts of a war of defence. But this has absolutely no influence upon the tactics of the Social Democracy.

From a *historical* standpoint the new German imperialism is, as we already know, absolutely aggressive. Urged onward by the feverish development of the national industry, German imperialism disturbs the old balance of power between the states and plays the first violin in the race for armaments.

And from the *standpoint of world politics* the present moment seemed to be most favourable for Germany to deal her rivals a crushing blow – which however does not lessen the guilt of Germany's enemies by one iota.

The diplomatic view of events leaves no doubt concerning the leading part that Germany played in Austria's provocative action in Serbia. The fact that Czarist diplomacy was, as usual, still more disgraceful, does not alter the case.

From the standpoint of *strategy* the entire German campaign was based on a monstrous offensive.

And finally from the standpoint of *tactics*, the first move of the German army was the violation of the Belgian neutrality.

If all this is defence, then what is attack? But even if we assume that events as pictured in the language of diplomacy admit of other interpretations – although the first two pages of the *White Book* are very clear as to their meaning – has the revolutionary party of the working class no other standards for determining its policy than the documents presented by a government that has the greatest interest in deceiving it:

"Bismarck duped the whole world," says Bebel, "and knew how to make people believe that it was Napoleon who provoked the war, while he himself, the peace-loving Bismarck, found himself and his policy in the position of being attacked.

"The events preceding the war were so misleading, that France's complete unpreparedness for the war, that she herself declared, was generally overlooked, while in Germany, which appeared to be the one attacked, preparations for war had been completed down to the very last wagon, and mobilization moved with the precision of clockwork." (*Autobiography*, Vol.III, pp.167-168).

After such an historical precedent one might expect more critical caution from the Social Democracy.

It is quite true that Bebel more than once repeated his assertion that in case of an attack on Germany the Social Democracy would defend its fatherland. At the convention held at Essen,[29] Kautsky answered him:

"In my opinion we cannot promise positively to share the government's war enthusiasm every time we are convinced that the country is threatened by attack. Bebel thinks we are much further advanced than we were in 1870 and that we are now able to decide in every instance whether the war which threatens is really one of aggression or not. I should not like to take this responsibility upon myself. I should not like to undertake to guarantee that we could make a correct decision in every instance, that we shall always know whether a government is deceiving us, or whether it is not actually representing the interests of the nation against a war of attack ... Yesterday it was the German government that took the aggressive, tomorrow it will be the French government, and we cannot know if the day after it may not be the English government. The governments are constantly asking turns. As a matter of fact what we are concerned with in case of war is not a national but an international question. For a war between great powers will become a world war and will affect the whole of Europe, not two countries alone. Some day the German government might make the German proletariat believe they were being attacked; the French government might do the same with its subjects, and then we should have a war in which the French and German working men would follow their respective governments with equal enthusiasm, and murder each other and cut each other's throats. Such a contingency must be avoided, and it will be avoided if we do not adopt the criterion of the aggressive or defensive war, but that of the interests of the proletariat, which at the same time are international interests ... Fortunately, it is a misconception to assume that the German Social

Democracy in case of war would want to judge by national and not by international considerations, and felt itself to be first a German and then a proletarian party.

With splendid clearness, Kautsky in this speech reveals the terrible dangers – now a still more terrible actuality – that are latent in the endeavour to make the position of the Social Democracy dependent upon an indefinite and contradictory formal estimate of whether a war is one of defence or one of aggression. Bebel in his reply said nothing of importance; and his point of view seemed quite inexplicable, especially after his own experience of the year 1870.

Nevertheless, in spite of its theoretical inadequacy, Bebel's position had a quite definite political significance. Those imperialistic tendencies which the danger of war begat excluded the possibility for the Social Democracy's expecting salvation from the victory of either of the warring parties. For that very reason its entire attention was directed to the preventing of war, and the principal task was to keep the governments worried about the results of a war.

"The Social Democracy," said Bebel, "Will oppose any government which takes the initiative in war." He meant his as a threat to Wilhelm II's government. "Don't reckon upon us if some day you decide to utilize your cannon and your battleships." Then he turned to Petrograd and London: "They had better take care not to attack Germany in a miscalculation of weakness from within on account of the obstructionist policy of the powerful German Social Democracy."

Without being a political doctrine, Bebel's conception was a political threat, and a threat directed simultaneously at two fronts, the internal front and the foreign front. His one obstinate answer to all historical and logical objections was: "We'll find the way to expose any government that takes the first step towards war. We are clever enough for that."

This threatening attitude of not only the German Social Democracy but also of the International Party was not without results. The various governments actually did make every effort to postpone the outbreak of the war. But that is not all. The rulers and the diplomats were doubly attentive now to adapting their moves to the pacifist psychology of the masses. They whispered with the Socialist leaders, nosed about in the office of the International, and so created a sentiment which made it possible for Jaurès and Haase to declare at Brussels, a few days before the outbreak of the War, that their particular governments had no other object than the preservation of peace.[30] And when the storms broke loose, the Social Democracy of every country looked for the guilty party – on the other side of the border. Bebel's utterance, which had played a definite part as a threat, lost all weight the instant the first shots were fired at the frontiers. That terrible thing took place which Kautsky had prophesied.

What at first glance appeared the most surprising thing about it all is, that the Social Democracy had not really felt the need for a political criterion. In the catastrophe that has occurred to the International the arguments have been notable for their superficiality. They contradicted each other, shifted ground, and were of only secondary significance the gist of the matter being that the father-land must be defended. Apart from considerations of the historical outcome of the War, apart from considerations of democracy and the class struggle, the fatherland that has come down to us historically must be defended. And defended not because our government wanted peace and was "perfidiously attacked", as the international penny-a-liners put it, but because apart from the conditions or the ways in which it was provoked, apart from who was right and who was wrong, war, once it breaks out, subjects every belligerent to the danger of invasion and conquest. Theoretical, political, diplomatic and military considerations fall into ruins as in an earthquake, a conflagration or a flood. The government with its army is elevated to the position of the one power that can protect and save its people. The large masses of the people in actuality return to a pre-political condition. This feeling of the masses, this elemental reflex of the catastrophe, need not be criticized in so far as it is only a temporary feeling. But is quite a different matter in the case of the attitude of the Social Democracy, the responsible political representative of the masses. The political organizations of the possessing classes and especially the power of the government itself did not simply float with the stream. They instantly set to work most intensively and in very varied ways to heighten this unpolitical sentiment and to unite the masses around the army and the government. The Social Democracy not only did not become equally active in the opposite direction, but from the very first moment surrendered to the policy of the government and to the elemental feeling of the masses. And instead of arming these masses with the weapons of criticism and distrust, if only passive criticism and distrust, it itself by its whole attitude hastened the people along the road to this pre-political condition. It renounced its traditions and political pledges of fifty years with a conspicuous readiness that was least of all calculated to inspire the rulers with respect.

Bethmann-Hollweg announced that the German government was in absolute agreement with the German people, and after the avowal of the *Vorwaerts*, in view of the position taken by the Social Democracy, he has a perfect right to say so. But he had still another right. If conditions had not induced him to postpone polemics to a more favourable moment, he might have said at the Reichstag session of August 4th, addressing the representatives of the Socialist proletariat:

"Today you agree with us in recognizing the danger threatening our fatherland, and you join us in trying to avert the danger by arms. But this danger has not grown up since yesterday. You must previously have known of the existence and the tendencies of Czarism, and you knew that we had other enemies besides. So by what right did you attack us when we built up our army and our navy? By what right did you refuse to vote for military appropriations year after year? Was it by the right of treason or the right of blindness? If in spite of you we had not built up our army, we should now be helpless in the face of this Russian menace that has brought you to your senses, too. No appropriations granted now could enable us to make up for what we would have lost. We should now be without arms, without cannons, without fortifications. Your voting today in favour of the war credit of five billions is an admission that your annual refusal of the budget was only an empty demonstration, and, worse than that, was political demagogy. For as soon as you came up for serious historical examination, you denied your entire past!"

That is what the German Chancellor could have said, and this time his speech would have carried conviction. And what could Haase have replied?

"We never took a stand for Germany's disarmament in the face of dangers from without. Such peace rubbish was never in our thoughts. As long as international contradictions create out of themselves the danger of war, we want Germany to be safe against foreign invasion and servitude. What we are trying for is a military organisation which cannot – as can an artificially trained organization be made to serve for class exploitation at home and for imperialistic adventures abroad, but will be invincible in national defence. We want a militia. We cannot trust you with the work of national defence. You have made the army a school of reactionary training. You have drilled your corps of officers in the hatred of the most important class of modern society, the proletariat. You are capable of risking millions of lives, not for the real interests of the people, but for the selfish interests of the ruling minority, which you veil with the names of national ideals and state prestige. We do not trust you, and that is why we have declared year after year, Not a single man or a single penny for this class government!'

"But five billions!" voices from both the right and the left might interrupt.

"Unfortunately we are now left no choice. We have no army except the one created by the present masters of Germany, and the enemy stands without our gates. We cannot on the instant replace Wilhelm II's army by a people's militia, and once this is so, we cannot refuse food, clothing and materials of war to the army that is defending us, no matter how it may be constituted. We are neither repudiating our past nor renouncing our future. We are forced to vote for the war credits."

That would have been about the most convincing thing that Haase could have said.

Yet, even though such considerations might give an explanation of why the Socialist workers as citizens did not obstruct the military organization, but simply fulfilled the duty of citizenship forced upon them by circumstances, we should still be waiting in vain for an answer to the principal question: Why did the Social Democracy, as the political organization of a class that has been denied a share in the government, as the implacable enemy of bourgeois society, as the republican party, as a branch of the International why did it take upon itself the responsibility for acts undertaken by its irreconcilable; class enemies?

If it is impossible for us immediately to replace the Hohenzollern army with a militia, that does not mean that we must now take upon ourselves the responsibility for the doings of that army. If in times of peaceful normal state-housekeeping we wage war against the monarchy, the bourgeoisie and militarism, and are under obligations to the masses to carry on that war with the whole weight of our authority, then we commit the greatest crime against our future when we put this authority at the disposal of the monarchy, the bourgeoisie and militarism at the very moment when these break out into the terrible, anti-social and barbaric methods of war. Neither the nation nor the state can escape the obligation of defence. But when we refuse the rulers our confidence we by no means rob the bourgeois state of its weapons or its means of defence and even of attack as long as we are not strong enough to wrest its powers from its hands. In war as in peace, we are a party of opposition, not a party of power. In that way we can also most surely serve that part of our task which war outlines so sharply, the work of national independence. The Social Democracy cannot let the fate of any nation, whether its own or another nation, depend on military successes. In throwing upon the capitalist state the responsibility for the method by which it protects its independence, that is, the violation of the independence of other states, the Social Democracy lays the cornerstone of true national independence in th consciousness of the masses of all nations. By preserving and developing the international solidarity of the workers, we secure the independence of the nation – and make it independent of the calibre of cannons.

If Czarism is a danger to Germany's independence, there is only one way that promises success in warding off this danger, and that way lies with us – the solidarity of the working masses of Germany and Russia. But such solidarity would undermine the policy that Wilhelm II explained in saying that the entire German people stood behind him. What should we Russian Socialists say to the Russian working men in face of the fact that the bullets the German workers are shooting at them bear the political and moral seal of the German Social Democracy? "We cannot make our policy for Russia, we make it for Germany," was the answer given me by one of the most respected functionaries of the German party when I put this question to him. And at that moment I felt with particularly painful clearness what a blow had been struck at the International from within.

The situation, it is plain, is not improved if the Socialist parties of both warring countries throw in their fate with the fate' of their governments, as in Germany and France. No outside power, no confiscation or destruction of Socialist property, no arrests and imprisonments could have dealt such a blow to the International as it struck itself with its own hands in surrendering to the Moloch of the state just when he began to talk in terms of blood and iron.

In his speech at the convention at Essen Kautsky drew a terrifying picture of brother rising against brother in the name of a "war of defence", as an argument, by no means as an actual possibility. Now that this picture has bec6me a bloody actuality, Kautsky endeavours to reconcile us to it. He beholds no collapse of the international.

"The difference between the German and the French Socialists is not to be found in their standards of judgement, nor in their fundamental point of view, but merely in the difference of their interpretation of the present situation, which, in its turn, is conditioned by the difference in their geographical position(!). Therefore, this difference can scarcely be overcome while the War lasts. Nevertheless it is not a difference of principle, but one arising out of a particular situation, and so it need not last after that situation has ceased to exist." (*Neue Zeit*, 337, p.3.)

When Guesde and Sembat appear as aides to Poincaré, Delcasse and Briand, and as opponents to Bethmann-Hollweg; when the French and German working men cut each other's throats and are not doing so as enforced citizens of the bourgeois republic and the Hohenzollern Monarchy, but as Socialists performing their duty under the spiritual leadership of their parties, this is not a collapse of the International. The "standard of judgement" is one and the same for the German Socialist cutting a Frenchman's throat as for the French Socialist cutting a German's throat. If Ludwig Frank takes up his gun, not to proclaim the "difference of principle" to the French Socialists, but to shoot them in all agreement of principle; and if Ludwig Frank should himself fall by a French bullet – fired possibly by a comrade – that is no detriment to "standards" they have in common. It is merely a consequence of the "difference in their geographical position". Truly, it is bitter to read such lines, but doubly bitter when they come from Kautsky's pen.

The International was opposed to the war.

"If, in spite of the efforts of the Social Democracy, we should have war," says Kautsky, "then every nation must save its skin as best it can. This means for the Social Democracy of every country the same right and the same duty to participate in its country's defence, and none of them may make of this a cause for casting reproaches (!) at each other." (*Neue Zeit*, p.7.)

Of such sort is this common standard to save one's own skin, to break one another's skulls in self-defence, and not to "reproach" one another for doing so.

But will the question be answered by the agreement in the standard of judgement? Will it not rather be answered by the quality of this common standard of judgement? Among Bethmann-Hollweg, Sazonov, Grey and Delcasse you also find agreement in their standards. Nor is there any difference of principle between them either. They least of all have any right to cast reproaches at each other. Their conduct simply springs from "a difference in their geographical position." Had Bethmann-Hollweg been an English Minister, he would have acted exactly as did Sir Edward Grey. Their standards are as like each other as their cannon, which differ in nothing but their calibre. But the question for us is, can we adopt their standards for our own?

"Fortunately, it is a misconception to assume that the German Social Democracy in case of war would want to judge by national and not by international considerations, and felt itself to be first a German and then a proletarian party."

So said Kautsky in Essen. And now when the national point of view has taken hold of all the working men's parties of the international in place of the international point of view that they held in common, Kautsky not only reconciles himself to this "misconception", but even tries to find in it agreement of standards and a guarantee of the rebirth of the International.

"In every national state the working class must also devote its entire energy to keeping intact the independence and the integrity of the national territory. This is an essential of democracy, that basis necessary to the struggle and the final victory of the proletariat." (*Neue Zeit*, 337, p.4.)

But if this is the case, how about the Austrian Social Democracy" Must it, too, devote its entire energy to the preservation of the non-national and anti-national Austro-Hungarian Monarchy? And the German Social Democracy? By amalgamating itself politically with the German army, it not only helps to preserve the Austro-Hungarian national chaos, but also facilitates the destruction of Germany's national unity. *National unity is endangered not only by defeat but also by victory.*

From the standpoint of the European proletariat it is equally harmful whether a slice of French territory is gobbled up by Germany, or whether France gobbles up a slice of German territory. More over the preservation of the European *status quo* is not a thing at all for our platform. The political map of Europe has been drawn by the point of the bayonet, at every frontier passing over the living bodies of the nations. If the Social Democracy assists its national (or anti-national) governments with all its energy, it is again leaving it to the powder and intelligence of the bayonet to correct the map of Europe. And in tearing the International to pieces, the Social Democracy destroys the one power that is capable of setting up a program of national independence and democracy in opposition to the activity of the bayonet, and of carrying out this program in a greater or lesser degree, quite independently of which of the national bayonets is crowned with victory.

The experience of old is confirmed once again. If the Social Democracy sets national duties above its class duties, it commits the greatest crime not only against Socialism, but also against the interest' of the nation as rightly and broadly understood.

Chapter VII.
The Collapse of the International

At their Convention in Paris two weeks before the outbreak of the catastrophe, the French Socialists insisted on pledging all branches of the International to revolutionary action in case of a mobilization. They were thinking chiefly of the German Social Democracy. The radicalism of the French Socialists in matters of foreign policy was rooted not so much in international as national interests. The events of the War have now definitely confirmed what was clear to many then. What the French Socialist Party desired from the sister party in Germany was a certain guarantee for the inviolability of France. They believed that only by thus insuring themselves with the German proletariat could they finally free their own hands for a decisive conflict with national militarism.

The German Social Democracy, for their part, flatly refused to make any such pledge. Bebel showed that if the Socialist parties signed the French resolution, that would not necessarily enable them to keep their pledge when the decisive moment came. Now there is little room for doubt that Bebel was right. As events have repeatedly proved, a period of mobilization almost completely cripples the Socialist Party, or at least precludes the possibility of decisive moves. Once mobilization is declared, the Social Democracy finds itself face to face with the concentrated power of the government, which is supported by a powerful military apparatus that is ready to crush all obstacles in its path and has the unqualified cooperation of all bourgeois parties and institutions.

And of no less importance is the fact that mobilization wakes up and brings to their feet those elements of the people whose social significance is slight and who play little or no political part in times of peace. Hundreds of thousands, nay millions of petty hand-workers, of hobo-proletarians (the riff-raff of the workers), of small farmers and agricultural labourers are drawn into the ranks of the army and put into a uniform, in which each one of these men stands for just as much as the class-conscious working man. They and their families are forcibly torn from their dull unthinking indifference and given an interest in the fate of their country. Mobilization and the declaration of war awaken fresh expectations in these circles whom our agitation practically does not reach and whom, under ordinary circumstances, it will never enlist. Confused hopes of a change in present conditions, of a change for the better, fill the hearts of these masses dragged out of the apathy of misery and servitude. The same thing happens as at the beginning of a revolution, but with one all-important difference. A revolution links these newly aroused elements with the revolutionary class, but war links them – with the government and the army! In the one case all the unsatisfied needs, all the accumulated suffering, all the hopes and longings find their expression in revolutionary enthusiasm; in the other case these same social emotions temporarily take the form of patriotic intoxication. Wide circles of the working class, even among those touched with Socialism, are carried along in the same current.

The advance guard of the Social Democracy feels it is in the minority; its organizations, in order to complete the organization of the army, are wrecked. Under such conditions there can be no thought of a revolutionary move on the part of the Party. And all this is quite independent of whether the people look upon a particularly war with favour or disfavour. In spite of the colonial character of the Russo-Japanese war and its unpopularity in Russia, the first half year of it nearly smothered the revolutionary movement. Consequently it is quite clear that, with the best intentions in the world, the Socialist parties cannot pledge themselves to obstructionist action at the time of mobilization, at a time, that is, when Socialism is more than ever politically isolated.

And therefore there is nothing particularly unexpected or discouraging in the fact that the working-class parties did not oppose military mobilization with their own revolutionary mobilization. Had the Socialists limited themselves to expressing condemnation of the present War, had they declined all responsibility for it and refused the vote of confidence in their governments as well as the vote for the war credits, they would have done their duty at the time. They would have taken up a position of waiting, the oppositional character of which would have been perfectly clear to the government as well as to the people. Further action would have been determined by the march of events and by those changes which the events of a war must produce on the people's consciousness. The ties binding the International together would have been preserved, the banner of Socialism would have been unstained. Although weakened for the moment, the Social Democracy would have preserved a free hand for a decisive interference in affairs as soon as the change in the feelings of the working masses came about. And it is safe to assert that whatever influence the Social Democracy might have lost by such an attitude at the beginning of the War, it would have regained several times over once the inevitable turn in public sentiment had come about.

But if this did not happen, if the signal for war mobilization was also the signal for the fall of the International, if the national labour parties fell in line with their governments and the armies without a single protest, then there must be deep causes for it common to the entire International. It would be futile to seek these causes in the mistakes of individuals, in the narrowness of leaders and party committees. They must be sought in the conditions of the epoch in which the Socialist International first came into being and developed. Not that the unreliability of the leaders or the bewildered incompetence of the Executive Committee should ever be justified. By no means. But these are not fundamental factors. These must be sought in the historical conditions of an entire epoch. For it is not a question and we must be very straightforward with ourselves about this – of any particular mistake, not of any opportunist steps, not of any awkward statements in the various parliaments, not of the vote for the budget cast by the Social Democrats of the Grand Duchy of Baden,[31] not of individual experiments of French ministerialism, not of the making or unmaking of this or that Socialist career. It is nothing less than the complete failure of the International in the most responsible historical epoch, for which all the previous achievements of Socialism can be considered merely as a preparation.

A review of historical events will reveal a number of facts and symptoms that should have aroused disquiet as to the depth and solidarity of Internationalism in the labour movement.

I am not referring to the Austrian Social Democracy. In vain did the Russian and Serbian Socialists look for clippings from articles on world politics in the *Wiener Arbeiter-Zeitung* that they could use for Russian and Serbian working men without having to blush for the International. One of the most striking tendencies of this journal always was the defence of Austro-German imperialism not only against the outside enemy but also against the internal enemy – and the *Vorwaerts* was one of the internal enemies. There is no irony in saying that in the present crisis of the International the *Wiener Arbeiter-Zeitung* remained truest to its past.

French Socialism reveals two extremes – an ardent patriotism, on the one hand, not free from enmity of Germany; on the other hand, the most vivid anti-patriotism of the Hervé type, which, as experience teaches, readily turns into the very opposite.

As for England, Hyndman's Tory-tinged patriotism, supplementing his sectarian radicalism, has often caused the International political difficulties.

It was in far less degree that nationalistic symptoms could be detected in the German Social Democracy. To be sure, the opportunism of the South Germans grew up out of the soil of particularism, which was German nationalism in octavo form. But the South Germans were rightly considered the politically unimportant rear-guard of the party. Bebel's promise to shoulder his gun in case of danger did not meet with a single-hearted reception. And when Noske repeated Bebel's expression, he was sharply attacked in the party press. On the whole the German Social Democracy adhered more strictly to the line of internationalism than any other of the old Socialist Parties. But for that very reason it made the sharpest break with its past. To judge by the formal announcements of the party and the articles in the Socialist press, there is no connection between the Yesterday and Today of German Socialism.

But it is clear that such a catastrophe could not have occurred had not the conditions for it been prepared in previous times. The fact that two young parties, the Russian and the Serbian, remained true to their international duties is by no means a confirmation of the Philistine philosophy, according to which loyalty to principle is a natural expression of immaturity. Yet this fact leads us to seek the causes of the collapse of the Second International in the very conditions of its development that least influenced its younger members.

Notes For Part II

25. A mining town in Alsace which had not been completely Germanized since annexation (1870), was the scene of friction between the army and the people in 1913. Lt. Baron von Forstner had insulted the French Flag while drilling recruits. The story leaked out and the recruits were arrested on a charge of betraying military secrets. On November 10, 1913, crowds were fired upon by German troops and Forstner called upon them to give miners a hot time.
26. In the time of Augustus, 9 AD, a Roman legion led by Varus was completely crushed by Herman's Teutons in the Teutoburger Forest.
27. Refers to Bismarck's manoeuvres that precipitated the Franco-Prussian war of 1870.
28. Bismarck's Anti-Socialist Laws were put into operation even before they were passed by the Reichstag in October 1878. All extra-parliamentary activity of the Socialists was banned. The laws were repealed in 1890.
29. The Essen Convention of the German Social Democrats took place in 1907.
30. On the 29th July 1914, after a meeting of the International Socialist Bureau at Brussels a largely attended public meeting was addressed by Jaurès, the recognized leader of the French Socialists, and Haase, Chairman of the German Social Democracy and head of its Reichstag fraction. Jaurès demonstratively put his arm round Haase, to the applause of the audience.
31. In 1904, in the (South German) Baden Landtag, a coalition between the Social Democrats and the Liberals drafted and voted for a budget. This was the first time that any Socialists had voted for a capitalist budget.

Glossary of Names

August Bebel. See Part I, glossary of names.

Theobald von Bethmann-Hollweg (1856-1921). Chancellor of the German Empire 1909-1917.

Otto von Bismarck, see Part I glossary of names

Bonaparte, Louis (Napoleon III). See Part I glossary of names

Aristide Briand (1862-1932). Once a militant member of the French Socialist Party; fought Millerand and his "Ministerialism" but later became Minister of Education 1906-1909. Expelled from SP, he founded the Republican Socialist Party with Millerand (1911). Premier several times, especially October 1915-March 1917. Delegate to the League of Nations.

Bernhard von Bülow, Prince (1849-1929). German diplomat. German chancellor and Prime Minister of Prussia 1900-1909.

Hans Delbrück(1848-1929). German military historian. Member of Reichstag 1884-1890.

Theophile Delcasse (1852-1923). French Foreign Minister 1898-1905, 1914-1916. Promoted *Entente Cordiale* with British.

Arthur Dix(1875-1935). German journalist, writer and editor.

Émile Driant (1855-1916). French soldier, politician and novelist. Son-in-law of General Boulanger. First high-ranking French casualty of Battle of Verdun, 1916.

Erich von Falkenhayn (1861-1922). German officer. Chief of Staff 1914-1916.

Ludwig Frank (1874-1914). SD Reichstag member. Revisionist, leader of Baden Socialists. Voted for war credits and volunteered for service as private after August 4th. Killed at Baccarat in France soon after, was first MP to die in action. In December 1914 his Reichstag seat was occupied by a wreath.

Sir Edward Grey (1862-1933). Liberal MP from 1885. Foreign Secretary December 1905-May 1916. Author of the oft-quoted remark at the beginning of the war: "The lamps are going out all over Europe; we shall not see them lit again in our lifetime."

Jules Basile Guesde. See Part I glossary of names

Hugo Haase. See Part I glossary of names

Paul von Hindenburg. See Part I glossary of names

Hohenzollern Dynasty. See Part I glossary of names

Georg Irmer (1853-1931). German imperialist. Member of colonial service and later journalist. Governor of the Marshall Islands 1894-1897. German Consul-General in Australia 1907-1911.

Jean Auguste Jaurès. French Socialist leader. Founder and editor *L'Humanité* 1904-1914. Leading figure in the 2nd International. Anti-militarist. Assassinated by French officers on 31st July 1914, the eve of the War.

Karl Kautsky (1854-1938). German Social Democrat. Theoretician of German Social Democracy. Leader of the 2nd International. A pacifist-centrist in World War I. Later right-winger in the Independent Socialist Party (USPD). Rejoined Social Democracy. Died in exile.

Alexander von Kluck, General (1846-1934). Commander German First Army in World War I. Invaded Belgium and responsible for numerous atrocities.

Ferdinand Lassalle. See Part I glossary of names

Karl Liebknecht. See Part I glossary of names

Wilhelm Liebknecht. See Part I glossary of names

Franz von Liszt (1851-1919). German academic, jurist and politician. Member of Progressive People's Party. Member of Reichstag from 1912.

Erich Ludendorff (1865-1937). German officer. Served on both Western and Eastern Fronts. Became Hindenburg's Deputy Chief of Staff in 1916. Represented Germany during negotiations with Bolsheviks leading to Treaty of Brest-Litovsk. Became Commander in Chief on Western Front 1918, organised unsuccessful final German offensive.

Rosa Luxemburg. See Part I glossary of names

Georg Michaelis (1857-1936). German civil servant. German Chancellor July-November 1917.

Helmuth von Moltke. See Part I glossary of names

Gustav Noske (1868-1946). Right-wing Social Democratic member of Reichstag during World War I. Became Minister of Defence after the German Revolution in November 1918. Organised suppression of the Spartacist uprising in January 1919, during which Rosa Luxemburg and Karl Liebknecht were murdered by right-wing officers.

Raymond Poincaré (1860-1934). Premier of France 1912, 1922-24, 1926-29. President 1913-1920. Militarist.

Ludwig Quessel (1872-1930). German Social Democrat of the extreme Right (Imperialist) Wing. Revisionist. Reichstag 1912-18 and 1920-30. Member Weimar National Assembly 1919-20.

Sergei D Sazonov (1861-1927). Russian diplomat. Foreign Minister 1910-1916. Ambassador to London 1917.

Theodor Schiemann (1847-1921). German historian of Baltic German origin. Publisher. Lecturer at the Prussian Academy of War. Friend of the Kaiser.

Johann Baptist von Schweitzer (1833-1875). President, General Association of German Workers (1867-71). Intrigued with Bismarck. When exposed, 1872, expelled.

Marcel Sembat (1862-1922). French Socialist. Deputy from 1893. Chauvinist during War. Joined Cabinet of National Defence as Minister of Public Works August 1914-September 1917.

Albert Sudekum. See Part I glossary of names

Herman Wendell. Right Wing German Social Democrat.

Willhelm II. See Part I glossary of names

Wilhelm (1882-1951). Son of Wilhelm II, Crown Prince of Germany.

The War and the International
Part III.

Chapter VIII.
Socialist Opportunism

The Communist Manifesto written in 1847, closes with the words: "Workingmen of all countries, unite!" But this battle cry came too early to become a living actuality at once. The historical order of the day just then was the middle class revolution of 1848. And in this revolution the part that fell to the authors of the Manifesto themselves was not that of leaders of an international proletariat, but of fighters on the extreme left of the national Democracy.

The revolution of 1848 did not solve a single one of the national problems; it merely revealed them. The counter-revolution, along with the great industrial development that then took place, broke off the thread of the revolutionary movement. Another century of peace went by until recently the antagonisms that had not been removed by the revolution demanded the intervention of the sword. This time it was not the sword of the revolution, fallen from the hands of the middle class, but the militaristic sword of war drawn from a dynastic scabbard. The wars of 1859, 1864, 1866 and 1870 created a new Italy and a new Germany. The feudal caste fulfilled, in their own way, the heritage of the revolution of 1848. The political bankruptcy of the middle class, which expressed itself in this historic interchange of roles, became a direct stimulus to an independent proletarian movement based on the rapid development of capitalism…

In 1863 Lasalle founded the first political labour union in Germany32. In 1864 the First International was formed in London under the guidance of Karl Marx. The closing watchword of the Manifesto was taken up and used in the first circular issued by the International Association of Workingmen. It is most characteristic for the tendencies of the modern labour movement that its first organization had an international character. Nevertheless this organization was an anticipation of the future needs of the movement rather than a real steering instrument in the class struggle.

There was still a wide gulf between the ultimate goal of the International, the communist revolution, and its immediate activities, which took the form mainly of international cooperation in the chaotic strike movement of the workers in various countries. Even the founders of the International hoped that the revolutionary march of events would very soon overcome the contradiction between ideology and practice. While the General Council was giving money to aid groups of strikers in England and on the Continent, it was at the same time making classic attempts to harmonize the conduct of the workers in all countries in the field of world politics.

But these endeavours did not as yet have a sufficient material foundation. The activity of the First International coincided with that period of wars which opened the way for capitalist development in Europe and North America. In spite of its doctrinal and educational importance, the attempts of the International to mingle in world politics must all the more clearly have shown the advanced workingmen of all countries their impotence as against the national class state. The Paris Commune, flaring up out of the war, was the culmination of the First International.[33] Just as the Communist Manifesto was the theoretical anticipation of the modern labour movement, and the First International was the practical anticipation of the labour associations of the world, so the Paris Commune was the revolutionary anticipation of the dictatorship of the proletariat.

But only an anticipation, nothing more. And for that very reason it was clear that it is impossible for the proletariat to overthrow the machinery of state and reconstruct society by nothing but revolutionary improvisations. The national states that emerged from the wars created the one real foundation for this historical work, the national foundation. Therefore, the proletariat must go through the school of self-education.

The First International fulfilled its mission of a nursery for the National Socialist Parties. After the Franco-Prussian War and the Paris Commune, the International dragged along a moribund existence for a few years more and in 1872 was transplanted to America, to which various religious, social and other experiments had often wandered before, to die there.

Then began the period of prodigious capitalist development, on the foundation of the national state. For the labour movement this was the period of the gradual gathering of strength, of the development of organization, and of political possibilism, or opportunism.

In England the stormy period of Chartism34, that revolutionary awakening of the English proletariat, had completely exhausted itself ten years before the birth of the First International. The repeal of the Corn Laws (1846) and the subsequent industrial prosperity that made England the workshop of the world, the establishment of the ten-hour working day (1847), the increase of emigration from Ireland to America, and the enfranchisement of the workers in the cities (1867), all these circumstances, which considerably improved the lot of the upper strata of the proletariat, led the class movement in England into the peaceful waters of trade unionism and its supplemental liberal labour policies.

The period of possibilism, that is, of the conscious, systematic adaptation to the economic, legal, and state forms of national capitalism, began for the English proletariat, the oldest of the brothers, even before the birth of the International, and twenty years earlier than for the continental proletariat. If nevertheless the big English unions joined the International at first, it was only because it afforded them protection against the importation of strike breakers in wage disputes35.

The French labour movement recovered but slowly from the loss of blood in the Commune, on the soil of a retarded industrial growth, and in a nationalistic atmosphere of the most noxious greed for "revenge". Wavering between an anarchistic "denial" of the state and a vulgar-democratic capitulation to it, the French proletarian movement developed by adaptation to the social and political framework of the bourgeois republic.

As Marx had already foreseen in 1870, the centre of gravity of the Socialist movement shifted to Germany.

After the Franco-Prussian War, unified Germany entered upon an era similar to the one England had passed through in the twenty years previous: an era of capitalist prosperity, of democratic franchise, of a higher standard of living for the upper strata of the proletariat.

Theoretically the German labour movement marched under the banner of Marxism. Still in its dependence on the conditions of the period, Marxism became for the German proletariat not the algebraic formula of the revolution that it was at the beginning, but the theoretic method for adaptation to a national-capitalist state crowned with the "Prussian helmet". Capitalism, which had achieved a temporary equilibrium, continually revolutionized the economic foundation of national life. To preserve the power that had resulted from the Franco-Prussian War, it was necessary to increase the standing army. The middle class had ceded all its political positions to the feudal monarchy, but had entrenched itself all the more energetically in its economic positions under the protection of the militaristic police state. The main currents of the last period, covering forty-five years, are: victorious capitalism, militarism erected on a capitalist foundation, a political reaction resulting from the inter-growth of feudal and capitalist classes – a revolutionizing of the economic life, and a complete abandonment of revolutionary methods and traditions in political life. The entire activity of the

German Social Democracy was directed towards the awakening of the backward workers, through a systematic fight for their most immediate needs – the gathering of strength, the increase of membership, the filling of the treasury, the development of the press, the conquest of all the positions that presented themselves, their utilization and expansion. This was the great historical work of the awakening and educating of the "unhistorical" class.

The great centralized trade unions of Germany developed in direct dependence upon the development of national industry, adapting themselves to its successes in the home and the foreign markets, and controlling the prices of raw materials and manufactured products. Localized in political districts to adapt itself to the election laws and stretching feelers in all cities and rural communities, the Social Democracy built up the unique structure of the political organization of the German proletariat with its many-branched bureaucratic hierarchy, its one million dues-paying members, its four million voters, ninety-one daily papers and sixty-five party printing presses. This whole many-sided activity, of immeasurable historical importance, was permeated through and through with the spirit of possibilism.

In forty-five years history did not offer the German proletariat a single opportunity to remove an obstacle by a stormy attack, or to capture any hostile position in a revolutionary advance. As a result of the mutual relation of social forces, it was constrained to avoid obstacles or adapt itself to them. In this, Marxism as a theory was a valuable tool for political guidance, but it could not change the opportunist character of the class movement, which in essence was at that time alike in England, France and Germany. For all the undisputed superiority of the German organization, the tactics of the unions were very much the same in Berlin and London. Their chief achievement was the system of tariff treaties. In the political field the difference was much greater and deeper. While the English proletariat were marching under the banner of Liberalism, the German workers formed an independent party with a Socialist platform. Yet this difference does not go nearly as deep in politics as it does in ideological forms and the forms of organization.

Through the pressure that English labour exerted on the Liberal Party it achieved certain limited political victories, the extension of suffrage, freedom to unionise, and social legislation. The same was preserved or improved by the German proletariat through its independent party, which it was obliged to form because of the speedy capitulation of German liberalism. And yet this party, while in principle fighting the battle for political power, was compelled in actual practice to adapt itself to the ruling power, to protect the labour movement against the blows of this power, and to achieve a few reforms. In other words: on account of the difference in historical traditions and political conditions, the English proletariat adapted itself to the capitalist state through the medium of the Liberal Party; while the German proletariat was forced to form a party of its own to achieve the very same political ends. And the political struggle of the German proletariat in this entire period had the same opportunist character limited by historical conditions as did that of the English proletariat.

The similarity of these two phenomena so different in their forms comes out most clearly in the final results at the close of the period. The English proletariat in the struggle to meet its daily issues was forced to form an independent party of its own, without, however, breaking with its liberal traditions; and the party of the German proletariat, when the War forced upon it the necessity of a decisive choice, gave an answer in the spirit of the national-liberal traditions of the English labour party.

Marxism, of course, was not merely something accidental or insignificant in the German labour movement Yet there would be no basis for deducing the social-revolutionary character of the party from its official Marxist ideology.

Ideology is an important, but not a decisive factor in politics. Its role is that of waiting on politics. That deep-seated contradiction, which was inherent in the awakening revolutionary class on account of its relation to the feudal-reactionary state, demanded an irreconcilable ideology which would bring the whole movement under the banner of social revolutionary aims. Since historical conditions forced opportunist tactics, the irreconcilability of the proletarian class found expression in the revolutionary formulas of Marxism. Theoretically, Marxism reconciled with perfect success the contradiction between reform and revolution. Yet the process of historical development is something far more involved than theorizing in the realm of pure thought. The fact that the class which was revolutionary in its tendencies was forced for several decades to adapt itself to the monarchical police state, based on the tremendous capitalist development of the country, in the course of which adaptation an organization of a million members was built up and a labour bureaucracy which led the entire movement was educated – this fact does not cease to exist and does not lose its weighty significance because Marxism anticipated the revolutionary character of the future movement. Only the most naive ideology could give the same place to this forecast that it does to the political actualities of the German labour movement.

The German Revisionists were influenced in their conduct by the contradiction between the reform practice of the party and its revolutionary theories. They did not understand that this contradiction is conditioned by temporary, even if long-lasting circumstances and that it can only be overcome by further social development. To them it was a logical contradiction. The mistake of the Revisionists was not that they confirmed the reformist character of the party's tactics in the past, but that they wanted to perpetuate reformism theoretically and make it the only method of the proletarian class struggle. Thus, the Revisionists failed to take into account the objective tendencies of capitalist development, which by deepening class distinctions must lead to the Social Revolution a the one way to the emancipation of the proletariat. Marxism emerged from this theoretical dispute as the victor all along the line. But Revisionism, although defeated on the field of theory, continued to live, drawing sustenance from the actual conduct and the psychology of the whole movement. The critical refutation of Revisionism as a theory by no means signified its defeat tactically and psychologically. The parliamentarians, the unionists, the comrades continued to live and to work in the atmosphere of general opportunism, of practical specializing and of nationalistic narrowness. Reformism made its impress even upon the mind of August Bebel, the greatest representative of this period.

The spirit of opportunism must have taken a particularly strong hold on the generation that came into the party in the eighties, in the time of Bismarck's anti-Socialist laws and of oppressive reaction all over Europe. Lacking the apostolic zeal of the generation that was connected with the First International, hindered in its first steps by the power of victorious imperialism, forced to adapt itself to the traps and snares of the anti-Socialist laws, this generation grew up in the spirit of moderation and constitutional distrust of revolution. They are now men of fifty to sixty years old, and they are the very ones who are now at the head of the unions and the political organizations. Reformism is their political psychology, if not also their doctrine. The gradual growing into Socialism – that is the basis of Revisionism – proved to be the most miserable Utopian dream in face of the facts of capitalist development. But the gradual political growth of the Social Democracy into the mechanism of the national state has turned out to be a tragic actuality – for the entire race.

The Russian Revolution was the first great event to bring a fresh whiff into the stale atmosphere of Europe in the thirty five years since the Paris Commune. The rapid development of the Russian working class and the unexpected strength of their concentrated revolutionary activity made a great impression on the entire civilized world and gave an impetus everywhere to the sharpening of political differences. In England the Russian Revolution hastened the formation of an independent labour party. In Austria, thanks to special circumstances, it led to universal manhood suffrage. In France the echo of the Russian Revolution took the form of Syndicalism, which gave expression, in inadequate practical and theoretical form, to the awakened revolutionary tendencies of the French proletariat. And in Germany the influence of the Russian Revolution showed itself in the strengthening of the young Left wing of the party, in the rapprochement of the leading Centre to it, and in the isolation of Revisionism. The question of the Prussian franchise, this key to the political position of Junkerdom, took on a keener edge. And the party adopted in principle the revolutionary method of the general strike. But all this external shaking up proved inadequate to shove the party on to the road of the political offensive. In accordance with the party tradition, the turn toward radicalism found expression in discussions and the adoption of resolutions. That was as far as it ever went.

Chapter IX.
The Decline of the Revolutionary Spirit

Six or seven years ago a political ebb-tide everywhere followed upon the revolutionary flood-tide. In Russia the counter-revolution triumphed and began a period of decay for the Russian proletariat both in politics and in the strength of their organizations. In Austria the thread of achievements started by the working class broke off, social insurance legislation rotted in the government offices, nationalist conflicts began again with renewed vigour in the arena of universal manhood suffrage, weakening and dividing the Social Democracy. In England, the Labour Party, after separating from the Liberal Party, entered into the closest association with it again. In France the Syndicalists passed over to reformist positions. Gustave Hervé changed to the opposite of himself in the shortest time. And in the German Social Democracy the Revisionists lifted their heads, encouraged by history's having given them such a revenge. The South Germans perpetrated their demonstrative vote for the budget. The Marxists were compelled to change from offensive to defensive tactics. The efforts of the Left Wing to draw the party into a more active policy were unsuccessful. The dominating Centre swung more and more towards the Right, isolating the Radicals. Conservatism, recovering from the blows it received in 1905, triumphed all along the line.

In default of revolutionary activity as well as the possibility for reformist work, the party spent its entire energy on building up the organization, on gaining new members for the unions and for the party, on starting new papers and getting new subscribers. Condemned for decades to a policy of opportunist waiting, the party took up the cult of organization as an end in itself. Never was the spirit of inertia produced by mere routine work so strong in the German Social Democracy as in the years immediately preceding the great catastrophe. And there can be no doubt that the question of the preservation of the organizations, treasuries, People's Houses and printing presses played a mighty important part in the position taken by the fraction in the Reichstag towards the War. "Had we done anything else we would have brought ruin upon our organization and our presses," was the first argument I heard from a leading German comrade.

And how characteristic it is of the opportunistic psychology induced by mere organization work, that out of ninety-one Social Democratic papers not one found it possible to protest against the violation of Belgium. Not one! After the repeal of the anti-Socialist laws, the party hesitated long before starting its own printing presses, lest these might be confiscated by the Government in the event of great happenings. And now that it has its own presses, the party hierarchy fears every decisive step so as not to afford opportunity for confiscation.

Most eloquent of all is the incident of the *Vorwärts* which begged for permission to continue to exist on the basis of a new program indefinitely suspending the class conflict. Every friend of the German Social Democracy had a sense of profound pain when he received his issue of the central organ with its humiliating "By Order of Army Headquarters". Had the *Vorwärts* remained under interdiction, that would have been an important political fact to which the party later could have referred with pride. At any rate that would have been far more honourable than to continue to exist with the imprint of the general's boots on its forehead.

But higher than all considerations of policy and the dignity of the party stood considerations of membership, printing presses, organization. And so the *Vorwärts* now lives as two-paged evidence of the unlimited brutality of Junkerdom in Berlin and in Louvain, and of the unlimited opportunism of the German Social Democracy.

The Right wing stood more by its principles, which resulted from political considerations. Wolfgang Heine crassly formulated these principles of German Reformism in an absurd discussion as to whether the Social Democrats should leave the hall of the Reichstag when the members rose to cheer the Emperor's name, or whether they should merely keep their seats. "The creation of a republic in the German Empire is now and for some time to come out of the range of all possibility, so that it is not really a matter for our present policy." The practical results still not yet achieved may be reached, but only through cooperation with the liberal bourgeoisie. "For that reason, not because I am a stickler for form, I have called attention to the fact that parliamentary cooperation will be rendered difficult by demonstrations that needlessly *hurt the feelings* of the majority of the House."

But if a simple infringement of monarchical etiquette was enough to destroy the hope of reformist cooperation with the liberal middle class, then certainly the break with the bourgeois "nation" in the moment of national "danger" would have hindered, for years to come, not only all desired reforms, but also all reformist desires. That attitude that was dictated to the routinists of the party centre by sheer anxiety over the preservation of the organization was supplemented among the Revisionists by political considerations. Their standpoint proved in every respect to be more comprehensive and won the victory all over. The entire party press is now industriously acclaiming what it once heaped scorn upon, that the present patriotic attitude of the working class will win for them, after the War, the good will of the possessing classes for bringing about reforms.

Therefore, the German Social Democracy did not feel itself, under the stress of these great events, a revolutionary power with tasks far exceeding the question of widening the state's boundaries, a power that does not lose itself for an instant in the nationalistic whirl but calmly awaits the favourable moment for joining with the other branches of the International in a purposeful interference in the course of events. No, instead of that the German Social Democracy felt itself to be a sort of cumbersome train threatened by hostile cavalry. For that reason it subordinated the entire future of the International to the quite extraneous question of the defence of the frontiers of the class state because it felt itself first and foremost to be a conservative state within the state.

"Look at Belgium!" cries the *Vorwärts* to encourage the workmen-soldiers. The People's Houses there have been changed into army hospitals, the newspapers suppressed, all party life crushed out. [A sentimental correspondent of the *Vorwärts* writes that he was looking for Belgian comrades in the *Maison da Peuple* and found a German Army hospital here. And what did the *Vorwärts* correspondent want of his Belgian comrades? "To win them to the cause of the German people" – when Brussels itself had already been won "for the cause of the German people!"] And therefore hold out until the end, "until the decisive victory is ours." In other words, keep on destroying, let the work of your own hands be a terrifying lesson to you. "Look at Belgium," and out of this terror draw courage for renewed destruction.

What has just been said refers not to the German Social Democracy alone, but also to all the older branches of the International that have lived through the history of the last half century.

Chapter X.
Working Class Imperialism

There is one factor in the collapse of the Second International that is still un-clarified. It dwells at the heart of all the events that the Party has passed through.

The dependence of the proletarian class movement, particularly in its economic conflicts, upon the scope and the successes of the imperialistic policy of the state is a question which, as far as I know, has never been discussed in the Socialist press. Nor can I attempt to solve it in the short space of this work. So what I shall say on this point will necessarily be in the nature of a brief review.

The proletariat is deeply interested in the development of the forces of production. The national state created in Europe by the revolutions and wars of the years 1789 to 1870 was the basic type of the economic evolution of the past period. The proletariat contributed by its entire conscious policy to the development of the forces of production on a national foundation. It supported the bourgeoisie in its conflicts with alien enemies for national liberation; also in its conflicts with the monarchy, with feudalism and the church for political democracy. And in the measure in which the bourgeois turned to "law and order", that is, became reactionary, the proletariat assumed the historical task the bourgeoisie had left uncompleted. In championing a policy of peace, culture and democracy, as against the bourgeoisie, it contributed to the enlargement of the national market, and so gave an impetus to the development of the forces of production.

The proletariat had an equal economic interest in the democratizing and the cultural progress of all other countries in their relation of buyer or seller to its own country. In this resided the most important guarantee for the international solidarity of the proletariat both in so far as final aims and daily policies are concerned. The struggle against the remnants of feudal barbarism, against the boundless demands of militarism, against agrarian duties and indirect taxes was the main object of working-class politics and served, directly and indirectly, to help develop the forces of production. That is the very reason why the great majority of organized labour joined political forces with the Social democracy. Every hindrance to the development of the forces of production touches the trade unions most closely.

As capitalism passed from a national to an international-imperialistic ground, national production, and with it the economic struggle of the proletariat, came into direct dependence on those conditions of the world market which are secured by dreadnaughts and cannon. In other words, in contradiction of the fundamental interests of the proletariat taken in their wide historic extent, the immediate trade interests of various strata of the proletariat proved to have a direct dependence upon the successes or the failures of the foreign policies of the governments.

England long before the other countries placed her capitalist development on the basis of predatory imperialism, and she interested the upper strata of the proletariat in her world dominion. In championing its own class interests, the English proletariat limited itself to exercising pressure on the bourgeois parties which granted it a share in the capitalist exploitation of other countries. It did not begin an independent policy until England began to lose her position in the world market, pushed aside, among others, by her main rival, Germany.

But with Germany's growth to industrial world-importance, grew the dependence of broad strata of the German proletariat on German imperialism, not materially alone but also ideally. The *Vorwärts* wrote on August 11th that the German workingmen, "counted among the politically intelligent, to whom we have preached the dangers of imperialism for years (although *with very little success*, we must confess)" denounce Italian neutrality like the extremist chauvinists. But that did not prevent the *Vorwärts* from feeding the German workingmen on "national" and "democratic" arguments in justification of the bloody work of imperialism. (Some writers' backbones are as flexible as their pens.)

However, all this does not alter facts. When the decisive moment came, there seemed to be no irreconcilable enmity to imperialistic policies in the consciousness of the German workingmen. On the contrary, they seemed to listen readily to imperialist whisperings veiled in national and democratic phraseology. This is not the first time that Socialistic imperialism reveals itself in the German Social Democracy. Suffice it to recall the fact that at the International Congress in Stuttgart it was the majority of German delegates, notably the trade unionists, who voted against the Marxist resolution on the colonial policy.[36] The occurrence made a sensation at the time, but its true significance comes out more clearly in the light of present events. Just now the trade union press is linking the cause of the German working class to the work of the army with more consciousness and matter-of-factness than do the political organs.

As long as capitalism remained on a national basis, the proletariat could not refrain from cooperation in democratizing the political relations and in developing the forces of production through its parliamentary, communal and other activities. The attempts of the anarchists to set up a formal revolutionary agitation in opposition to the political fights of the Social Democracy condemned them to isolation and gradual extinction. But when the capitalist states overstep their national form to become imperialistic world powers, the proletariat cannot oppose this new imperialism. And the reason is the so-called minimal program which fashioned its policy upon the framework of the national state. When its main concern is for tariff treaties and social legislation, the proletariat is incapable of expending the same energy in fighting imperialism that it did in fighting feudalism. By applying its old methods of the class struggle – the constant adaptation to the movements of the markets – to the changed conditions produced by imperialism, it itself falls into material and ideological dependence on imperialism.

The only way the proletariat can pit its revolutionary force against imperialism is under the banner of Socialism. The working class is powerless against imperialism as long as its great organizations stand by their old opportunist tactics. The working class will be all-powerful against imperialism when it takes to the battlefield of Social Revolution.

The methods of national-parliamentary opposition not only fail to produce practical results, but also cease to make an appeal to the labouring masses, because the workers find that, behind the backs of the parliamentarians, imperialism, by armed force, reduces the wages and the very lives of the workers to ever greater dependence on its successes in the world market.

It was clear to every thinking Socialist that the only way the proletariat could be made to pass from opportunism to Revolution was not by agitation, but by a historical upheaval. But no one foresaw that history would preface this inevitable change of tactics by such a catastrophic collapse of the International. History works with titanic relentlessness. What is the Rheims Cathedral[37] to History? And what a few hundred or thousand political reputations? And what the life or death of hundreds of thousands or of millions?

The proletariat has remained too long in the preparatory school, much longer than its great pioneer fighters thought it would. History took her broom in hand, swept the International of the epigones apart in all directions and led the slow-moving millions into the field where their last illusions are being washed away in blood. A terrible experiment! On its result perhaps hangs the fate of European civilization.

Chapter XI.
The Revolutionary Epoch

At the close of the last century a heated controversy arose in Germany over the question, What effect does the industrialization of a country produce upon its military power? The reactionary agrarian politicians and writers, like Sehring, Karl Ballod, Georg Hansen and others, argued that the rapid increase of the city populations at the expense of the rural districts positively undermined the foundation of the Empire's military power, and they of course drew from it their patriotic inferences in the spirit of agrarian protectionism. On the other hand Lujo Brentano and his school championed an exactly opposite point of view. They pointed out that economic industrialism not only opened up new financial and technical resources, but also developed in the proletariat the vital force capable of making effective use of all the new means of defence and attack. He quotes authoritative opinions to show that even in the earlier experiences of 1870-71 "the regiments from the preponderantly industrial district of Westphalia were among the very best." And he explains this fact quite correctly by the far greater ability of the industrial worker to find his bearings in new conditions and to adjust himself to them.

Now which side is right? The present War proves that Germany, which had made the greatest progress along capitalist lines, was able to develop the highest military power. And likewise in regard to all the countries drawn into it the War proves what colossal and yet competent energy the working class develops in its warlike activities. It is not the passive horde-like heroism of the peasant masses, welded together by fatalistic submissiveness and religious superstition. It is the individualized spirit of sacrifice, born of inner impulse, ranging itself under the banner of the Idea.

But the Idea under whose banner the armed proletariat now stands, is the Idea of war-crafty nationalism, the deadly enemy of the true interests of the workers. The ruling class showed themselves strong enough to force their Idea upon the proletariat, and the proletariat, in the consciousness of what they were doing, put their intelligence, their enthusiasm and their courage at the service of their class foes. In this fact is sealed the terrible defeat of Socialism. But it also opens up all possibilities for a final victory of Socialism. There can be no doubt that a class which is capable of displaying such steadfastness and self-sacrifice in a war it considers a 'just" one, will be still more capable of developing these qualities when the march of events will give it tasks really worthy of the historical mission of this class.

The epoch of the awakening, the enlightenment and the organization of the working-class revealed that it has tremendous resources of revolutionary energy which found no adequate employment in the daily struggle. The Social Democracy summoned the upper strata of the proletariat into the field, but it also checked their revolutionary energy by adopting the tactics it was obliged to adopt, the tactics of waiting, the strategy of letting your opponent exhaust himself. The character of this period was so dull and reactionary that it did not allow the Social Democracy the opportunity to give the proletariat tasks that would have engaged their whole spirit of sacrifice.

Imperialism is now giving them such tasks. And imperialism attained its object by pushing the proletariat into a position of "national defence", which, to the workers, meant the defence of all their hands had created, not only the immense wealth of the nation, but also their own class organizations, their treasuries, their press, in short, everything they had unswervingly, painfully struggled for and attained in the course of several decades. Imperialism violently threw society off its balance, destroyed the sluice-gates built by the Social Democracy to regulate the current of proletarian revolutionary energy, and guided this current into its own bed.

But this terrific historical experiment, which at one blow broke the back of the Socialist International, carries a deadly danger for bourgeois society itself. The hammer is wrenched out of the worker's hand and a gun put into his hand instead. And the worker, who has been tied down by the machinery of the capitalist system, is suddenly torn from his usual setting and taught to place the aims of society above happiness at home and even life itself.

With the weapon in his hand that he himself has forged, the worker is put in a position where the political destiny of the state is directly dependent upon him. Those who exploited and scorned him in normal times, now flatter him and toady to him. At the same time he comes into intimate contact with the cannon, which Lassalle calls one of the most important ingredients of all constitutions.[38] He crosses the border, takes part in forceful requisitions, and helps in the transfer of cities from one party to another. Changes are taking place such as the present generation has never before seen.

Even though the vanguard of the working class knew in theory that Might is the mother of Right, still their political thinking was completely permeated by the spirit of opportunism, of adaptation to bourgeois legalism. Now they are learning from the teachings of facts to despise this legalism and tear it down. Now dynamic forces are replacing the static forces in their psychology. The great guns are hammering into their heads the idea that if it is impossible to get around an obstacle, it is possible to destroy it. Almost the entire adult male population is going through this school of war, so terrible in its realism, a school which is forming a new human type. Iron necessity is now shaking its fist at all the rules of bourgeois society, at its laws, its morality, its religion. "Necessity knows no law", said the German Chancellor on August 4th. Monarchs walk about in public places calling each other liars in the language of market-women; governments repudiate their solemnly acknowledged obligations; and the national church ties its God to the national cannon like a criminal condemned to hard labour. Is it not clear that all these circumstances must bring about a profound change in the mental attitude of the working class, curing them radically of the hypnosis of legality in which a period of political stagnation expresses itself?

The possessing classes, to their consternation, will soon have to recognize this change. A working class that has been through the school of war will feel the need of using the language of force as soon as the first serious obstacle faces them within their own country. "Necessity knows no law", the workers will cry when the attempt is made to hold them back at the command of bourgeois law. And poverty, the terrible poverty that prevails during this War and will continue after its close, will be of a sort to force the masses to violate many a bourgeois law. The general economic exhaustion in Europe will affect the proletariat most immediately and most severely. The state's material resources will be depleted by the War, and the possibility of satisfying the demands of the working masses will be very limited. This must lead to profound political conflicts, which, ever widening and deepening, may take on the character of a social revolution, the progress and outcome of which no one, of course, can now foresee.

On the other hand, the War with its armies of millions, and its hellish weapons of destruction can exhaust not only society's resources but also the moral forces of the proletariat. If it does not meet inner resistance, this War may last for several years more, with changing fortunes on both sides, until the chief belligerents are completely exhausted. But then the whole fighting energy of the international proletariat, brought to the surface by the bloody conspiracy of imperialism, will be completely consumed in the horrible work of mutual annihilation. The outcome would be that our entire civilization would be set back by many decades. A peace resulting not from the will of the awakened peoples but from the mutual exhaustion of the belligerents, would be like the peace with which the Balkan War was concluded; it would be a Bucharest Peace extended to the whole of Europe.

Such a peace would seek to patch up anew the contradictions, antagonisms and deficiencies that have led to the present War. And with many other things, the Socialist work of two generations would vanish in a sea of blood without leaving a trace behind.

Which of the two prospects is the more probable? This cannot possibly be theoretically determined in advance. The issue depends entirely upon the activity of the vital forces of society – above all upon the revolutionary Social Democracy.

"Immediate cessation of the War" is the watchword under which the Social Democracy can reassemble its scattered ranks, both within the national parties, and in the whole International. The proletariat cannot make its will to peace dependent upon the strategic considerations of the general staffs. On the contrary, it must oppose its desire for peace to these military considerations. What the warring governments call a struggle for national self-preservation is in reality a mutual national annihilation. Real national self-defence now consists in the struggle for peace.

Such a struggle for peace means for us not only a fight to save humanity's material and cultural possessions from further insane destruction. It is for us primarily a fight to preserve the revolutionary energy of the proletariat.

To assemble the ranks of the proletariat in a fight for peace means again to place the forces of revolutionary Socialism against raging tearing imperialism on the whole front.

The conditions upon which peace should be concluded – the peace of the people themselves, and not the reconciliation of the diplomats – must be the same for the whole International.

No Reparations.
The Right to every nation to Self-Determination.
The United Staes of Europe – Without Monachies, Without Standing Armies, Without Ruling Feudal Classes, Without Secret Diplomacy.

The peace agitation, which must be conducted simultaneously with all the means now at the disposal of the Social Democracy as well as those which, with a good will, it could acquire, will not only tear the workers out of their nationalistic hypnosis; it will also do the saving work of inner purification in the present official parties of the proletariat. The national Revisionists and the Socialist patriots in the Second International, who have been exploiting the influence that Socialism has acquired over the working masses for national militaristic aims, must be thrust back into the camp of the enemies of the working class by uncompromising revolutionary agitation for peace.

The revolutionary Social Democracy need not fear that it will be isolated, now less than ever. The War is making the most terrible agitation against itself. Every day that the War lasts will bring new masses of people to our banner, if it is an honest banner of peace and democracy. The surest way by which the Social Democracy can isolate the militaristic reaction in Europe and force it to take the offensive is by the slogan of Peace.

We revolutionary Marxists have no cause for despair. The epoch into which we are now entering will be our epoch. Marxism is not defeated. On the contrary: the roar of the cannon in every quarter of Europe heralds the theoretical victory of Marxism. What is left now of the hopes for a "peaceful" development, for a mitigation of capitalist class contrasts, for a regular systematic growth into Socialism?

The Reformists on principle, who hoped to solve the social question by the way of tariff treaties, consumers' leagues, and the parliamentary cooperation of the Social Democracy with the bourgeois parties, are now all resting their hopes on the victory of the "national" arms. They are expecting the possessing classes to show greater willingness to meet the needs of the proletariat because it has proved its patriotism.

This expectation would be positively foolish if there were not hidden behind it another, far less "idealistic" hope – that a military victory would create for the bourgeoisie a broader imperialistic field for enriching itself at the expense of the bourgeoisie of other countries, and would enable it to share some of the booty with its own proletariat at the expense of the proletariat of other countries. *Socialist reformism has actually turned into Socialist Imperialism.*

We have witnessed with our own eyes the pathetic bankruptcy of the hopes of a peaceful growth of proletarian well-being. The Reformists, contrary to their own doctrine, were forced to resort to violence in order to find their way out of the political *cul-de-sac* – not the violence of the peoples against the ruling classes, but the military violence of the ruling classes against other nations. Since 1848 the German bourgeoisie has renounced revolutionary methods for solving its problems. They left it to the feudal class to solve their own bourgeois questions by the method of war. Social development confronted the proletariat with the problem of revolution. Evading revolution, the Reformists were forced to go through the same process of historical decline as the liberal bourgeoisie. The Reformists also left it to their ruling classes, that is the same feudal caste, to solve the proletarian problem by the method of war. But this ends the analogy.

The creation of national states did really solve the bourgeois problem for a long period, and the long series of colonial wars coming after 1871 finished off the period by broadening the arena of the development of the capitalist forces. The period of colonial wars carried on by the national states led to the present War of the national states – for colonies. After all the backward portions of the earth had been divided among the capitalist states, there was nothing left for these states except to grab the colonies from each other.

"People ought not to be talking," says Georg Irmer, "as though it were a settled thing that the German nation has come too late for rivalry for world economy and world dominion that the world has already been divided. Has not the earth been divided over and over again in all epochs of history?"

But a redivision of colonies among the capitalist countries does no enlarge the foundation of capitalist development. One country's gain means another country's loss. Accordingly a temporary mitigation of class-conflicts in Germany could only be achieved by an extreme intensification of the class struggle in France and in England, and vice versa. An additional factor of decisive importance is the capitalist awakening in the colonies themselves, to which the present War must give a mighty impetus. Whatever the outcome of this War, the imperialistic basis for European capitalism will not be broadened, but narrowed. The War, therefore, does not solve the labour question on an imperialistic basis, but, on the contrary, it intensifies it, putting this alternative to the capitalist world: *Permanent War or Permanent Revolution.*

If the War got beyond the control of the Second International, its immediate consequences will get beyond the control of the bourgeoisie of the entire world. We revolutionary Socialists did not want the War. *But we do not fear it.* We do not give in to despair over the fact that the War broke up the International. History has already disposed of the International.

The revolutionary epoch will create new forms of organization out of the inexhaustible resources of proletarian Socialism, new forms that will be equal to the greatness of the new tasks. To this work we will apply ourselves at once, amid the mad roaring of the machine-guns, the crashing of cathedrals, and the patriotic howling of the capitalist jackals. We will keep our clear minds amid this hellish death music, our undimmed vision. We feel ourselves to be the only creative force of the future. Already there are many of us, more than it may seem. Tomorrow there will be more of us than today. And the day after tomorrow, millions will rise up under our banner, millions who even now, sixty seven years after the *Communist Manifesto*, have nothing to lose but their chains.

Notes For Part III

32. The General Association of German Workers was founded at Leipzig on 23rd March 1863. President: Ferdinand Lassalle (1825-1864); Vice-President: Dr. Otto Dammer; Secretary: Karl Julius Valteich, a shoemaker(1839-1915).
33. The Paris Commune. Following France's defeat in the war of 1870-71, the workers of Paris seized power. On March 28, 1871 the Commune was declared. It was drowned in blood May 21-28, 1871. Some 20,000 to 30,000 Communards, including women and children, were killed, 270 executed after "trial", 400 jailed, 7000 transported from the country. The Commune marked the end of monarchy in France and the beginning of the Third Republic. The International Workingmen's Association (the First International) was founded by Marx and Engels in 1864. In its "first phase" it served as the rallying point of various European national sections. After the Paris Commune, in 1872, the centre was moved to New York. It was dissolved in 1876.
34. Chartism. A British movement for parliamentary reform (universal male suffrage, annual parliaments, vote by ballot, payment of MPs, equal electorates, abolition of property qualification, etc.) began in 1838 as a campaign to collect signatures to the People's Charter. It had some violent episodes (24 killed at Manchester and Newport on November 3, 1839). had its ups and downs and flared up finally in April 1848.
35. In the Summer of 1866 British railway companies tried to import cheap Belgian labour. The First International committed itself to stop blacklegging. (See *Minutes of the General Council 1866-68*, p.333).
36. Although the Stuttgart Conference of the Second International (1907) was able to achieve unanimity on the attitude to war, on the colonial question it was sharply divided. An anti-colonial resolution was passed 127 to 108, with the Germans (though divided among themselves) voting solidly for the 'colonialists'.
37. In September 1914, the Cathedral of Rheims, where every French King from Clovis to Louis XVI had been crowned, was shelled by German guns.
38. Lassalle made his famous analysis of the essence of constitutions in a speech to a Berlin audience on April 16, 1862.

Glossary Of Names

Karl Ballod (1864-1931). Bourgeois economist. Professor University of Berlin from 1905.

August Bebel. See Part I glossary of names

Otto von Bismarck. See Part I glossary of names

Lujo Brentano (1844-1931). German economist, one of the "State" or "Professorial Socialists", who founded the Society for Social Politics in 1873 opposed to the Social Democracy.

Wolfgang Heine (1861-1944). German Social democrat. Lawyer. Prominent revisionist. Social chauvinist during World War I. Prussian Minister for justice November 1918-January 1919.

Gustave Hervé. See Part I glossary of names

Georg Irmer (1853-1931). German imperialist. Member of colonial service and later journalist. Governor of the Marshall Islands 1894-1897. German Consul-General in Australia 1907-1911.

Ferdinand Lassalle. See Part I glossary of names

Gregus on the Democratic List[1]

Since Russian censorship inhibits Russian liberalism from expressing its feelings of patriotic enthusiasm about the liberating mission of the Russian army, Mr Miliukov[2] took advantage, very felicitously, of an interviewer to bring to the attention of European public opinion his hopes and expectations.

This war has the task of "the destruction of militarism" and "the strengthening of the principles of democracy." This we have heard many times and moreover from different angles. But full confidence in the military triumph of democracy you get only when the voice in defense of it rises from the womb of Russian patriotism. At the end of the day, old parliamentary Britain, as events show again, has too small military resources to accomplish a liberation campaign on the European continent. It is scarcely possible to saddle republican France, with its population of 40 million, the task of restructuring and reshaping Europe. It is all the more comforting to hear from Mr. Miliukov, confirmation of the idea that tsarist Russia, with its inexhaustible human material - although, alas, in great financial difficulties - has taken upon itself "the destruction of militarism" and "the strengthening of the principles of democracy." The war, which is lead on the Russian side by the Grand Duke Nikolai, is essentially "a colossal revolution - against militarism and for the nation, against imperialism and for democracy" It is not clear who this program actually belongs to: Mr. Miliukov or the Grand Duke? If it is the Grand Duke, why does Miliukov personally have to impart this program ... in Italian? If it is only Miliukov, in what ways is it proposed to press the Russian army and Russian diplomacy into service? On this score Miliukov is unclear. "After this terrible bloody hurricane - he says - people have a firm right to peace and relief from the unbearable burden of armaments" We, however, do not think that the "right" of the peoples for peace and freedom from militarism should be strengthened by means of "a bloody hurricane". Regardless of this, what are the actual forces that will be called on to achieve the platonic right to peace? "The victorious democracies" – the liberal politician says - must force not only the belligerent countries involved in the war to disarm, but also the neutral. It almost looks like an answer, you need only to unwrap its content. "The victorious democracies", means France and England. But what about the victorious autocracy? Clearly it should be forced to disarm. The Cadet leader calls on France and Britain - otherwise he makes no sense - to forcibly disarm Tsarism. Here is a Russian liberal developing a revolutionary programme...in Italian!

In what way "the victorious democracies" will perform this task with respect to the victorious autocracy, again is not entirely clear. Tsarism will not be taken with bare hands. To carry out this programme, Miliukov suggests, in essence, a war of France and England against Russia - in order to ensure "the right to peace". Are we not fundamentally mistaken however, in our interpretation of Miliukov's thoughts? Does not Mr Miliukov also include among the victorious democracies tsarist Russia – using the same approach as the semi-official forerunner of Russian democracy, Sobakevitch, who included Elizaveta Vorobya in the list of souls of the male gender?[4] And is not this tradition of Sobakevich, the basic premise of all the liberal-patriotic speculation of Miliukov, in Italian, as well as in Russian? The most august Elizaveta Vorobya would have a lot to laugh into his beard about on this account, if cruel nature had not robbed him, among many other gifts, of the gift of irony.

Apparently Mr. Miliukov felt that somehow all this was not coming across very smoothly, or perhaps the interviewer Magrini suggested the idea to him. The Cadet leader saw himself forced from the perspectives of international pacifism and international democracy to the shortcomings of the internal system... "On the eve of war - admits Milyukov - the Russian people were filled with a discontent that was expressed with great energy... There was disorder on the streets, caused by huge strikes". Were the causes of this dissatisfaction eliminated? Miliukov dare not assert this. But he claims - and with some justification - something different: "all Russia's discontent that accumulated against the bureaucracy, found an outlet against Germany: it was opened like a big drain". In other words, Miliukov acknowledges that the war rendered a great service to the cause of reaction, allowing our ongoing internal danger to hide behind the external peril and directing popular discontent onto the wrong track. In short, militant reaction deceived the people. However, not all the people. We know about the actions of the Social Democratic deputies and Trudoviki, about the illegal proclamations, the response to Vandervelde, and the arrest of the Social Democratic Conference.[5] Finally, our "Voice" arose not by chance, it reflects the sentiments and views of a certain section of people. Who is Miliukov with: those who cheat, or those who expose the deception? He is with those who want to be deceived, in order to retain his ability to help deceive them. After all, this is generally the modest historical role of Russian liberalism!

Sticking to his brief, the leader of Russian liberalism says to the Italians that "after the war, the Russian government will be forced to bow to the necessary democratic reforms". Why exactly? "An ally of France and Britain, the Russian nation is waging a war in defense of democratic principles. How can it be that these principles are not victorious in the country?" Absolutely correct: a government leading a war in the interests of democracy, above all would ensure these principles triumphed in their own country. But that's why it is an absurd and shameful lie to claim that the tsarist government is able to wage war in the name of "democratic principles". That the conquest of Galicia, Persia, Armenia, Constantinople and the Straits serve the development of Russian capitalism, there is no doubt. But on this basis it is not democracy that will flourish but militant imperialism, which with an iron sheaf of fire will expand its objectives to the Balkans, Central and South Asia and the Far East.

Even the Italian interviewer, apparently, was not fully satisfied with a democratic cheque for an uncertain future signed by Mr Miliukov. He was interested in the situation now. What news is there about Poland, Finland, the Caucasus and the Jews? But here the liberal leader immediately wilted. "You can imagine" that Poland will get the promised autonomy. We, in any case, will "plead" for the autonomy of Finland, where at present Bobrikovsky measures are being introduced, that at one time even frightened Plehve.[6] "Maybe" the Caucasus can achieve autonomy. The Jews? "Unfortunately, among the soldiers in Poland powerful anti-Semitic propaganda is being seen. The Jews are accused of espionage". And this is the entire down-payment under democracy?

No, not at all. Miliukov has a trump card. "The greatest victory we have gained over the Germans is - the destruction of alcoholism". What have the Germans got to do with it - We ask ourselves perplexed? Is this an allusion to Count von Witte, the father of the liquor monopoly and head of the Germanophile party at court? Not at all. It would be wrong to look for any clues in this phrase, as well as for ideas in general. One of the objectives of the war is in fact, as we already know, to direct grievances that have accumulated against the bureaucracy, into a new "sewer" - against Germany. Russian liberalism took it upon itself to be one of the conduits. In relation to this, it is necessary in passing, to reject as ballast, even those five kopeck truths advanced by the liberals at the anti-alcohol congress: that with mere bans nothing is achieved, that it is necessary to raise the cultural level of the masses, that space is needed for people's initiative, etc., etc. If nothing is said about this, the Italian will probably never guess that the Russian artisan is now drinking denatured alcohol and polish.

We have still not exhausted the whole interview, and have already long felt uneasy over that political level with which it is necessary to hold the reader. This accursed time future historians will denounce not only as an era of brutality and savagery, but also as the era of stupidity and hypocrisy. Both of these traits are not accidental, they reflect the tremendous disparity between the war and the whole of culture created by mankind. Caught by surprise by the resurgence of the most shocking barbarism, individuals, parties and nations stupidly or hypocritically adapt still not forgotten concepts and terminology of a complex culture, to the facts of bloody plunder and mass murder. Russian liberalism is not an exception, but it is in a more difficult position. Since the historical nature of Tsarism is manifested in this war with incomparable brilliance in Lemberg,[7] as well as in Petrograd, Russian liberalism, in its apologetics, has had to use up exorbitant amounts of both ideological "substances": hypocrisy and stupidity.

- You see - says Mr. Milyukov, to European public opinion, here is our public minded Gregus from Riga. Previously, he was in our torture department and roasted the heels of imprisoned democrats with state supplied candles. And now we have transferred him to Lemberg, and the same state-owned candles in his hands will be called upon to play a role as beacons of democracy. Peoples have the right to peace and freedom from militarism. Neither will produce Gregus, a murderer on the Democratic list.

Notes

1. *The Voice, (Golos)*, December 10, 1914. First translation into English. Gregus was a notorious guard, who tortured prisoners in Riga after the revolution of 1905.
2. Pavel Miliukov was the leader of the Constitutional Democratic Party in Russia, or Cadets He was the most prominent Russian liberal and supported the war. Trotsky is commenting on an interview he gave to an Italian paper.
3. As well as being Commander in Chief, the Grand Duke was an ultra-reactionary and supporter of the Black Hundred anti-semitic murder gangs.
4. A reference to characters in Gogol's book, *Dead Souls*. Sobakevitch, a greedy corrupt landlord, sold a female serf or soul, passing her off as a man, thereby increasing her value, by the simple expedient of removing the 'a' from the end of her name. The suffix 'a' denotes female gender in Russian.
5. Eleven Social Democrats, six Mensheviks and five Bolsheviks refused to vote for war credits in the Duma. The Trudoviks, a peasant party, also refused. Emile Vandervelde was a prominent socialist leader in Belgium who joined the government at the outbreak of the war. He wrote to the Social Democratic deputies in the Duma calling on them to support the war. The Bolshevik deputies replied denouncing him. The Tsarist authorities subsequently raided a conference of the Bolsheviks in Petrograd and arrested those present.
6. Nikolai Bobrikov was a former Governor General of Finland when it was part of the Tsarist empire. He was notorious for the wave of repression and Russification he unleashed against the Finnish people. Assassinated in 1904 by a Finnish nationalist. Vyacheslav von Plehve was head of the Tsarist secret police and then Interior minister. Ultra-reactionary. Also assassinated in 1904, this time by the Socialist Revolutionary Party.
7. Present-day Lviv in the Ukraine. Lemberg had recently been captured, although temporarily, by the Russians. Also, see following paragraph in the text.

In the Balkans[1]

The fight of the European military powers, without a decisive advantage to one side or another, is reflected in the Balkans in the form, unprecedented even for this battle-scarred peninsula, of chaos cravings, plans, plots, schemes and intrigues.

Whilst the bourgeois parties in the great capitalist powers sharply oppose each other in national affairs, they consider it a matter of class honor to have agreement and continuity in matters of international policy, but with the small, isolated and always dependent Balkan States the opposite is the case. The local bourgeois parties hardly differ at all from each other in domestic politics. The need to escape from their economic and especially military backwardness, under the pressure of European capital, imposes on all the Balkan parties in power the same simple policy: loans, tax increases, the construction of railways, the development of militarism, increased taxes, borrowing. But in foreign policy, the ruling parties in the Balkans are sharply divided into two camps, depending on with which of the two main rivals in the Balkans, Russia or Austria, or the two major European groupings, they are ready to a greater or lesser extent, to unite their destinies.

Deceived in 1879 by Russia,[2] Romania before the war was primarily in the orbit of Austria and Germany. Squeezed by Austro-Hungary, Serbia gravitated towards Russia, since it was sufficiently remote and therefore less dangerous. Finally, equidistant from Russia and Austria, Bulgaria conducted a policy of manoeuvring between the two, promoting, alternately, Russophile and Austrophile parties to government posts. The war left in operation the previous forces of attraction and repulsion, but undermined those abject elements of resistance, which you could still find in Balkan politics in the era of the armed peace of the Great Powers. The choice of an "international" path now takes the form of a question in each of the Balkan countries, i.e. which of the political chieftains will seize power in these heated and uncertain times?

That's why European cabinets now take such an interest - and this is far from being only a platonic interest - in each extra vote for Venizelos,[3] in the internal struggles which

Romanian conservatives wage against Romanian liberals, and whether Gennadiev[4] will end up as Minister-President or in prison. The inevitable M. Hervé[5] threatens finally to give up on the Bulgarians, if they sew an ace of diamonds[6] to the back of their newly converted friend, the Quadruple Entente.[7] From time to time M. Clemenceau[8] composes an ode in honour of the "great European", Take Ionescu,[9] standing at the head of the party of social scum and of candidates hungry to be plunderers of the state.

The intervention of Italy into the war tipped the scales in Bulgaria in favour of the Allies, in line with the increased chances of the victory of the Quadruple Alliance. Not to mention the old Russophile parties, who, since the beginning of the war, were pushing Bulgaria to intervene, part of the traditional Russophobe Stambulists,[10] showed a desire to enter into negotiations with the Quadruple Alliance. The former Chief of the Stambulists, the aforementioned Gennadiev, in twenty-four hours turned from being an Austrian agent to a friend of Russia: you have to believe that he was presented with sufficiently convincing arguments. According to the plan, already seemingly close to implementation, Bulgaria - *L'État du Destin* (the country of destiny) - was supposed to open the way for Russia to Constantinople and for this to get Adrianople and part of Macedonia. But the surrender of Pržemyšl and Lemberg cooled the "Quadruple's" enthusiasm and again strengthened the chances of the stick-insect Radoslavov,[11] whose Government intends to remain neutral – until the moment when the collapse of Serbia will give it the opportunity with minimum risk to go into Macedonia. Anyway, hope for Bulgaria to join the Allies should now be considered to have suffered a complete collapse.

Russian defeat, then, not only made the expected intervention by Romania problematical, but also allowed Austria to present to the Bucharest government a demand, a reply to be given within a month, on which of the two factions she intends to support. For the "Great Europeans" of Romania however, the period of a month may prove to be too short to find out who will be the winner and therefore who, for sure, they can or cannot support.

While the Russian failure totally paralysed Bulgaria and Romania, the effect of the Italian military intervention, the results of which are manifesting themselves extremely slowly, created extraordinary difficulties on the western half of the Balkans. Fearing that Italy, having captured Istria and Dalmatia, will lay her hands on them, Serbia and Montenegro, almost completely shutting down military operations against Austria, sent their forces against Albania: whether to directly reward themselves at her expense, or to be able to exchange it for Dalmatia. In any event, in complete contradiction with the general plans of their "great" allies, at least the Western ones. In this infernal game where all national programmes, class egotisms, dynastic interests and factional intrigues clash head to head, the Balkan Social Democracy has again been put to the test and is maintaining its program as the only party of the future - a program that does not rely on rapid and fleeting constellations of diplomatic and military powers, but on the drive for general economic development.

It is difficult to imagine a picture more ugly than the cowardly and lustful politics of Balkan governments, who look into the eyes of the Great Powers afraid of being cheated, but with the intent to defraud. They also look suspiciously at each other, unable to form a solid alliance, but always ready for betrayal. Perhaps more outrageous is the Balkan policy of the Great Powers who buy and barter their allies, like gypsies at a horse fair.

Clemenceau, with utter contempt, says that the Balkan peoples do not know what they want. This is both true and untrue. The Balkan peoples most certainly want M. Clemenceau, his friends, and his enemies to leave them in peace. But they don't really know how to achieve this. However, the more the world war reveals the total impossibility of the Balkan governments' squabbling, the more it should clear the way for a single programme for the national and governmental co-existence of the Balkan peoples.

To the question of whether Bulgaria could tie its fate to the Quadruple Alliance, the theoretical organ of the Bulgarian social democracy, "Novo Vreme", replied in the negative. The main task for Russia is Constantinople and the Straits. England and France are now interested - not politically but strategically - to open a way out for Russia to the Mediterranean Sea as soon as possible. Otherwise in winter, when the port of Archangel will again be closed, Russia will be totally cut off from her Western allies. With Bulgarian help, Russia will take Constantinople and the surrounding area, and to protect the latter, she will then need the key to Constantinople, Adrianople. Russia as the master of the Black Sea coast and the Sea of Marmara - so argues the Bulgarian Social-Democratic organ - means the imminent loss of national independence of Bulgaria and Romania. The triumph of the Quadruple Alliance on the other side, means the consolidation of Italy on the Adriatic coast, where it will take the place of Austria. The Balkan states, corroded by rivalry, will be so hopelessly hemmed in between Russia and Italy, they will remember the old pre-liberation era with envy.

The Bulgarian Social Democracy gives, of course, a not less negative reply to the question of a union with the Central Empires. Their victory would mean in practice the replacement of weak Turkey by all-powerful Germany and Serbia would be taken over by Austro-Hungary. Bulgaria, today separate from the Great Powers, will be squeezed in their vice. The independent existence the Balkan peoples will come to an end.

It is precisely here in the Balkans, where great and small-power politics have their most naked character, where national and imperialist issues are intertwined in a terrible tangle, that the contradictions of social-nationalism emerge in their most naked form. Whichever of the two principles you take: defence of the fatherland or the search for the least misfortune internationally, they both turn out equally hopeless. How can you protect the fatherland: with Russia, which will devour you? With Germany, which will swallow you? With a cowardly and unstable neutrality, which events and the appetites of the rulers could dislodge at anytime? Which of the possible lines of government policy should the Social Democracy support? Precisely because all the issues of world politics confront the Balkan Social Democracy in such a bare form, in each section, the slogan of "defence of the homeland" was removed right at the dawn of its existence. It was replaced with a slogan to overcome the isolation and jealousy of these close, but weak states - by the introduction of a broader, viable community, a Balkan Republican Federation.

Struggling against the intervention of Bulgaria and Romania into the war on the side of one combination or the other, the Bulgarian and the Romanian sections of the Balkan International do not, however, stand for the stagnant state policy of "neutrality", of temporising impotence. Along with the courageous Serb party, they defend the principles of active democratic politics, leading to the union of all Balkan peoples.

Even if now, in this bloody intoxication, this program has a mostly propagandist character - in a revolutionary period, it will very soon put on flesh and blood, quickly wearing down all other programs and illusions and the more deeply Social Democracy will consolidate its authority, given by its political and moral courage, in the minds of the Balkan masses.

Notes

1. Published in *Nashe Slovo, (Our Word)*, July 20, 1915. First translation into English.
2. In the Russian -Turkish war of 1877, Romania fought on the side of Russia, but Russia subsequently seized Bessarabia, then in Romania, now part of Moldova.
3. Eleftherios Venizelos (1864-1936). Prime Minister of Greece during the war.
4. Gennadiev was a former Bulgarian Minister of Commerce, who was involved in a famous corruption scandal.
5. Gustave Hervé (1871-1944) Former pacifist socialist, became ultra-nationalist politician during WW1.
6. The ace of diamonds is a reference to the marking on the back of convicts' uniforms in tsarist Russia, in this context indicating a sign of betrayal.
7. The Quadruple Entente was the grouping in the war lead by France and Britain.
8. George Clemenceau was the leading capitalist politician of the French Third Republic. He was out of office at the time this article was written.
9. Take Ionescu (1858-1922) Leader of the Romanian Conservative Democratic Party, pushed to join the war on the side of Britain and France.
10. The Stambulists were the main anti-Russia party in Bulgaria at the time.
11. Vasil Radoslavov, (1858-1923), Prime Minister of Bulgaria, supported joining the war on the side of Germany and Austria.

'The Home Front'[1]

The Russian press, with the same spiritual poverty as the Ostyak[2] whose song is exhausted in five or six words, talks day after day about "the mobilization of industry" and "the organisation of social forces."

The supreme focus of this mobilization and organization should be the military-civic committee,[3] but its main characteristic remains complete uncertainty of its tasks, composition and powers: it is neither a subsidiary body under the war ministry, nor a supra-governmental organ of the parliamentary dictatorship, a committee of public salvation.

It would seem everyone agrees on only one thing, the mobilization of forces and the military-civic committee should both be to confront the enemy. This is the politics of the "home front": to the extent that the bourgeois opposition is showing signs of life, it remains entirely on a patriotic basis. In the meantime, the mobilisation of social forces is being carried out in the name of more effective "national defence", so that one could say that Guchkov and Miliukov have committed political plagiarism of Plekhanov, if only Plekhanov's entire position was not in itself a dismal borrowing from Miliukov and Guchkov.[4]

By the mobilization of industry is understood its adaptation to military needs and the fulfilment of state orders, so that the army would receive as much ammunition and military equipment as possible. They have taken Britain as their model. They have however closed their eyes to the fact that in Britain it is a matter of adapting the mightiest, and of its kind, most perfected capitalist organisation, with the flexibility of a democratic state apparatus, to the needs of the war. Even there experience has shown that it was much slower than expected or promised at the outset. Here, the issue is of technical, economic and governmental improvisation: the creation of a well-established network of railways, new plant, intelligent and technologically trained personnel, and not of thieving officials, etc. It is utopian to expect the technical and cultural leap forward needed to confront a German line of Mausers and bayonets.

The government itself cannot fail to understand this, for it knows better than anyone, how completely it has let itself get stuck in the patriotic cart. For the government, the matter is therefore mainly one of transferring real and direct economic responsibility for the war onto the propertied classes that previously had full political responsibility for it. In response, the parties and possessing class demand, without, however, any energy or persistence, not power, but a closer proximity to its sources: political, administrative and financial. The government has by no means promised this, but at the same time neither has it completely closed the door. This pretence of rapprochement is proceeding in line with the classic model of the late Svyatopolk-Mirsky's "Spring".[5] With almost virginal reticence, the "public figures" reply with timid gestures, the press choir pleads for "trust",- in short, performing once more the entire ritual of hypocrisy and stupidity, as if after the "Spring" of Svyatopolk-Mirsky, 9th January 1905 and 1905 in general had never happened. They act as if the world had never experienced the first two Dumas and June 3, 1907,[6] and ultimately, as if the same cast of characters, now grown mangy and having lost their last teeth, had not been standing on the stage for the past ten years.

The Committee of National Defence must become the centre of power in society, and the focus of a national mobilization against the external enemy. But what then should the Ministry be? In the nature of things, it would seem, it should play the role of the Committee of National Defence. Meanwhile it intends, after relinquishing a good share of responsibility, to more certainly remain at the bureaucratic centre of power. All the rumours about the appointment of the brothers Guchkov and Volkonsky[7] and others as ministers, proved to be premature. The purging of the whole of Galicia[8] has not been enough to cleanse the bureaucracy of even two or three ministerial jobs. So far the matter has been limited to the appointment of "public figures" to the Advisory Commission.

Meanwhile if the bureaucracy is not rushing to clear out posts, the so-called public figures are in no hurry to extend a helping hand to them. The "non-partisan" left press accuses Miliukov of insufficient urgency in demanding the convocation of the State Duma and the establishment of the Committee of National Defence. But what can Miliukov look for in the Duma now? There he will have to pledge his trust in the government, rather than call it to account. The notorious military-civic committee can give him still less: in taking on direct practical responsibility for the organisation of defence, the Cadet party would close the last opening in which it can still act out its opposition, between State policy and its material-technical resources and methods. It is precisely into this the gap that Plekhanov and our other social-patriots have attempted to drive the policy of the party of the proletariat.

However, social democracy can as little join the "home front" of Nikolai Nikolaevich,[9] as it can be seen as an ally of the armies of Hindenburg, holding the ministerial doors ajar to the parties of national liberalism. That terrible "criticism of arms", which is taking place on the Russian Western front, is limited to the weapons themselves, i.e. the military-technical fruits of the government regime. Ideological and material criticism of the regime as a whole, now more than ever in the past, lies with the Russian proletariat

Notes

1. From *Nashe Slovo, (Our Word)*, July 22, 1915. First Translation from Russian. .
2. The Ostyaks, since the 1930s called the Khanty, are an indigenous people of Western Siberia.
3. Became known as the Central War Industries Committee.
4. Miliukov and Guchkov were leaders of the conservative, pro-war Constitutional Democrat Party (Cadet) and Octobrist parties, respectively. Georgi Plekhanov is generally acknowledged as the founder of Russian Marxism, but in 1914 took a pro-war position, leading to Lenin calling him a social chauvinist.
5. P D Svyatopolk-Mirsky (1857-1914). Minister of the Interior in Russia, 1904-5. Politically associated with the Dowager Empress, Maria Fyoderovna, who took a slightly less reactionary position than her son, Tsar Nicholas II. 'Spring' is a reference to some minor reforms Svyatopolk-Mirsky proposed in 1904, that were rejected out of hand.
6. As Interior Minister, Svatapolk-Mirsky carried out the Tsar's order to massacre peaceful protesters outside the Winter Palace in St Petersburg on 9th January 1905, heralding the start of the first Russian Revolution. As a result of the revolution, a representative body was convened in 1906 known as the First Duma, that was however quickly suppressed. The Second Duma, of 1907, with greater left wing representation, was also short lived, being dissolved after 42 days in office on June 3rd 1907.
7. Volkonsky, V. M.(1868-?). Member of the third and forth Dumas. In summer 1915, under the influence of military defeats, Volkonsky was appointed an advisor of the Minister of the Interior.
8. Galicia is in present day western Ukraine. At the beginning of the war, although the Russian army was defeated in the north, it succeeded in pushing the Austro-Hungarian forces out of Galicia. However, in June 1915, the Austrians retook the area.
9. Grand Duke Nikolai Nikolaevich, (1856-1929). Commander in Chief of the Russian armies on the main front in the first year of the war.

A Convention of Confusion and Impotence[1]

Square brackets [] indicate material removed by the censor. Where the text was re-inserted in later editions this is shown inside these brackets

Since Russia began the so-called "social mobilization", which is still characterized by a complete formlessness of goals and methods, references to the control by parliament that our "democratic" allies benefit from, have played a clinching role in the columns of the Russian liberal press. But the wiles of historical development have organised it so that the present struggle to establish and renew parliamentary control in France is fed by references, very flattering to our national pride, to the parliamentary freedom of the State Duma. Not only Senator Ember, but Clemenceau and his henchman Hervé, recommend a republican democracy inspired by the high standards of the Bobrinsky and Savenko group in ensuring the triumph of the national will against the inertia of the bureaucracy and the partisan claims of capitalist cliques.[2]

This system of mutual back-scratching is further complicated by the fact that, inspired by French parliamentarism, Russian liberalism now mostly shrugs off the question of ministerial responsibility, without which parliamentary control is transformed into three-quarters empty ritualism. On the other hand, French Radicals appeal not only to the practice of the Third of June Duma, but to the traditions of the revolutionary wars and the Committee of Public Safety.[3] In all this confusion of ideas there is not only a mockery of a sense of history, but also a profound political lesson for those who have no reason to ignore or violate the meaning of history. French bourgeois democracy inherited the parliamentary regime from the epoch of the Great Revolution, and an appeal to the latter is an important factor in the semi-official phraseology of the Republic. Yet the historical development of the last decades has finally undermined the social fabric of democracy. Imperialism is not compatible with it. And since it was stronger, it emptied it out. Formally, universal suffrage produces parliament, and parliament produces the government. However, the government now has got into the mess of secret diplomatic obligations and bank influence, and does the will of finance capital, which in the elections barely showed its political face. Clemenceau is unhappy with the impotence of parliament[....]. Although the Jacobins are completely alien to Clemenceau, nevertheless, in utopian thought, capitalist imperialism is subordinated to the regime of democracy, so he wants to only preserve the shell of democracy, the rejection of which would be too risky an experiment for the French bourgeoisie. At the same time he tries to use parliamentary mechanics to combat the excesses or deficiencies of militarism when he, Clemenceau, is not in power himself. But in the end, in such a political reckoning of the inheritance of 1792, there is nothing fundamentally unacceptable even for the people of June 3rd, our original parliamentarians, Uncle Mitya and Uncle Minya,[4] who, switching their seats from a horse in the shafts to an outrider, try to drag the deeply mired state cart along the road..

Consequently, no matter how paradoxically, there are reciprocal links of "responsible" politicians from the Seine and the Neva. But in these links there is substantially more political significance than hope, held by our homeland mountain Democrats,[5] that Russia's military cooperation with France and Britain means the introduction into the body Tsarism of elements of parliamentary democracy.

But Russian imperialism came too early, or Russian parliamentarism too late - the people of June 3rd had no revolutionary ancestors who left them a legacy of a parliamentary regime. [It was not granted, therefore to our imperialists to conceal their appetites behind revolutionary traditions and a carefully drawn backdrop of popular sovereignty. The people of June 3rd, through the fault of their forebears, must, in internal and external politics, take to the field stark naked]. For seven years Miliukov[6] remained on the doorstep of the Commission of National Defence, but nevertheless zealously hid the whole of Russian militarism from the country's population. For five years Guchkov6 headed the commission itself, and could not even affect the size of the bribes of the commissariat. Each of these "people's representatives", in their field, prepared the current war and prepared Russia for the war. Miliukov dared to express the Jacobin idea relating to the Minister of War who "cheated the Duma" (it truly wanted to be cheated), that it will not be enough to put him out on an excellent pension, he needs to be brought to justice. Also, he instilled hope that Guchkov, as the Carnot[7] of the 3rd of June, will deliver the ammunition needed to evacuate Vilna and Riga and will publicly speak about the dangers of the new renaming of Petersburg as Petrograd. Imperialists to the bone, they primarily wanted victory, one that would give them Galicia and Armenia, Constantinople and the Straits, and along with the Straits, the entire Balkan Peninsula. [But it turned out that their forebears not only didn't bequeath them parliamentarism, but a great deal else, including the conditions for military victory. Abandoning the struggle for power and responsible ministries in the name of victory, the people of June 3rd more surely brought down defeat on their heads. And they accepted it. Military defeats are better than revolution, which is pregnant with social defeat]. True, the people of June 3rd found in the figure of Kerensky a patriotic revolutionary radical who wants to link a program for victory with the program of the democratic revolution. Two or three successful oratorical gestures could not, however, cover the basic futility of his position. If those classes who are interested in victory fear revolution more than defeat, then the class which is the main force of the revolution, connects the fate of Russian democracy not with the fate of national arms, but with the fate of the revolutionary struggle of the international proletariat.

In contrast to Kerensky, Chkheidze, who also spoke in the Duma, expelled Mankov[8] from the Social Democratic fraction. If Miliukov complements Clemenceau, then Mankov is a translation of Sembat[9] into the language of Eastern Siberia, not to mention San Remo (G V Plekhanov[10] lived in San Remo. *L. T.*). If the sly Clemenceau refers to the parliamentary energy of the IV Duma, the simpleton Mankov refers to the example of Anglo-French socialists fighting against German militarism. But, alas! His ancestors didn't leave Mankov a legacy of democratic forms of government, behind which he could conceal the content of the imperialist war. That's why Mankov is not only a Far-Eastern complement to pan-European social-nationalism, but is its pitiable caricature.

A convention of confusion and impotence! - This is the true face of the new Duma session. But out of the confusion of the rulers sometimes grow big events. Only for big events to lead to big results in the development of the country, it is necessary that the confusion of the rulers is surmounted by the determination and strength of those ruled-over and deceived.

Notes

1. From *Nashe Slovo, (Our Word)*, August 18th, 1915. First Translation into English.
2. Ember was a member of the French Upper House of Parliament, the Senate. He was very critical of France's military preparations for the war. Georges Clemenceau was the leading politician in the 3rd Republic, founded after the Paris Commune in 1871. He refused to serve in the government at the beginning of the war, eventually becoming Prime Minister in 1917. Gustave Hervé was the founder of La Guerre Sociale- a French Socialist newspaper. It was anti-war until 29th July 1914. Subsequently took an extreme social chauvinist position. Bobrinsky and Savenko were leading parliamentary figures supporting the Black Hundreds. The Black Hundreds were anti-semitic murder gangs, sponsored by Tsar Nicholas II.
3. As a result of the 1905 revolution, a representative body was convened in 1906 known as the First Duma, that was however quickly suppressed. The Second Duma, of 1907, with greater left wing representation, was also short lived, being dissolved after 42 days in office on June 3rd 1907. The Committee of Public Safety was formed in 1793 during the French Revolution. It formed the effective executive body of the government. The People of June 3rd is a reference to the regime and its supporters installed after the dissolution of the 2nd Duma.

4. Uncle Mitya and Uncle Minya. - characters from Gogol's "Dead Souls" - village men, who, wanting to help pull Chichkov's cart, switch from a horse in the shafts to an out-rider.
5. The rather obscure reference to 'mountain democrats' could refer to a Russian Social Democratic deputy, mentioned later in the article, who switched from an internationalist to a social-chauvinist position, and came from a mountainous region of Siberia. It could also be ironically linking this deputy with the Mountain of the French Revolution, the elevated section of seating in the Convention where the Jacobins sat, a name by which they became known.
6. Miliukov and Guchkov were leaders of the conservative, pro-war Constitutional Democrat Party (Cadet) and Octobrist parties, respectively.
7. Lazare Carnot, a leading figure in the French Revolution, main organiser of the revolutionary armies.
8. N V Chkheidze was a Menshevik, who, at the outset of the war, adopted a centrist or vacillating position, sometimes opposing the war. Later supported the war. I Mankov was a member of the Menshevik fraction in the Duma from Eastern Siberia, who was expelled from Chkheidze's group after making a pro-war speech in the IV Duma.
9. Marcel Sembat, a one-time left member of the French Socialist Party who joined the government on the outbreak of the war.
10. G V Plekhanov was the founder of Russian Marxism, who took a pro-war position in 1914, leading Lenin to denounce him as a social chauvinist.

A Year of War[1]

Square brackets [] indicate material removed by the censor. Where the text was re-inserted in later editions this is shown inside these brackets

The past year - three hundred sixty-five days and nights of continuous mutual extermination of the peoples - will go down in our history as a staggering testament to how deeply humanity is still imprisoned in shameful blind barbarism by its social roots.

In order to stigmatize the German Mausers, which have a bigger diameter than the Allied guns, and the German shells, which spread their suffocating stench further than those of the *Quadruple Entente*,[2] Allied rhetoric created a special term, barbarie scientifique or 'scientific barbarism'. The perfect term! It is only necessary to extend it to the entire war and its socio- historical background - regardless of state and national borders. All those technical forces that created human progress moved to the business of the destruction of the cultural foundations of society, and, above all, of the annihilation of mankind: this is the "mobilization of industry", which is now spoken about in all the languages of European civilization. Educated barbarism is armed with all the conquests of human genius - from Archimedes to Edison - to erase from the surface of the earth everything created by humanity collectively, by Archimedes and Edison. If the Germans stand out in this bloody, insane competition, it is only because they are more widely, systematically and efficiently organized than their mortal enemies.

As if to give the fall of mankind the most humiliating character, the war, using the latest proud technological conquest of aviation, has driven man into trenches, into dirty earthen caves, sewers, where the rulers of nature, eaten away by parasites, lying in their own filth, lie in wait for other troglodytes, covered with lice, and newspapers and politicians in various languages, all say that it is precisely this, that is now serving civilization. Crawling on all fours from the dark primordial swamp, humanity brought its organised mind to bear in the struggle with nature. By heroic revolutionary upheavals, it brought elements of reason to state structures, displacing blind inertia, "by the Grace of God", with the idea of popular sovereignty and a parliamentary regime. But in the very foundations of its social life, in its economic organization, humanity remains entirely in the grip of dark forces, beyond rational control, which are always threatening to spontaneously explode with accumulated contradictions and then bring them down onto the head of mankind, in the form of global catastrophes.

Europe, torn by capitalist development from medieval provincialism and economic inertia, in a series of revolutions and wars, created incomplete 'national' states, from both large and small powers, and linked them in a transient and ever-changing scheme of antagonisms alliances and agreements. Nowhere having achieved national unity, capitalist development came into conflict with the state framework it had created, and for the last half-century sought a way out in continuous colonial plunder, leading, untypical for Europe, to an 'armed peace'. This system, in which the ruling upper classes economically, politically and psychologically adapted themselves to the monstrous growth of militarism, gave birth to a war for world domination - the most colossal and shameful war that history has known.

The war has already involved seven of the eight great powers and threatens to involve the eighth;[3] in order to broaden its base, it draws in the minor powers one after the other (all the work of diplomacy now consists of this). It automatically dissolves individual subordinate aims into the mechanics of mutual debilitation, exhaustion and extermination. With the generality, formlessness and multiplicity of its aims, combining and throwing against each other all races and nationalities, all state systems and all stages of capitalist development, this war of usurpation wants to show that it is completely free from any racial or national origins, religious or political principles - it simply expresses the bare fact of the impossibility of the further coexistence of peoples and states on the basis of capitalist imperialism.

The system of alliances, as it developed after the Franco-Prussian War, was generated by a desire to create a guarantee of stability of states through a rough military balance of opposing forces. This equilibrium, demonstrated by the current guerre d'usure (war of attrition), precludes the possibility of a fast and decisive victory of one party and makes the outcome of the war dependent on the gradual depletion of the approximately equal material and moral resources of the opponents.

On the western front, the thirteenth month of the war finds the trenches in about the same place they were in the second month. Here they have moved tens of metres in either direction - through the bodies of thousands and tens of thousands of soldiers. On the Gallipoli Peninsula, as well as on the new Austro-Italian front, the lines of trenches immediately signified lines of military hopelessness. On the Russian -Turkish border it is the same picture on a provincial scale. Only on the eastern (Russian) front, giant armies, after a series of movements in both directions, now roll back to the east onto the body of ravaged Poland, which each party promises to "liberate".

In this picture, [generated by the blind automatism of capitalist forces and the conscious shame of the ruling classes], there are absolutely no points of reference that, from a military point of view, would allow, in any way whatsoever, any hopes and plans to be linked with a decisive victory for either side. If the ruling powers of Europe had had as much historical good intent as bad, then they would still have been powerless by force of arms to resolve the problems that caused the war. [The strategic situation in Europe gives a mechanical expression to the historical impasse, into which the capitalist world has driven itself].

Even if the socialist parties were powerless to prevent the war in its first period, or to hold the rulers to account, if from the outset they had declined to take any responsibility for the global carnage, and the parties had used their close links to warn the people against the rulers and to denounce them, played a waiting game - in the sense of revolutionary action - counting on the inevitable turn in the mass mood - how great would now have been the authority of international socialism to the masses. Deceived by militarism, weighed down by mourning and increasing want, all the more would the masses have turned their eyes to the true shepherd of the peoples! Look! In a condition of desperation, both groups of military powers are now grasping for every small state: Romania, Bulgaria or Greece, for the L'État du Destin ("the country of destiny"), whose weight could finally tip the balance in one direction or another. What really would be a "make or break" weight under these conditions is the International, the great power of international socialism, whose every word would find an ever greater echo in the minds of the masses! The liberation program, which individual sections of the broken International are now dragging through the bloody filth in the tail of the General Staff baggage train, would become a powerful reality in an international approach of the socialist proletariat against all the forces of the old society.

But history, even at this time, remained stepmother to the oppressed class. Its national parties incorporated into their organizations not only the initial successes of the proletariat, not only its desire for total liberation, but also all of the indecision of the oppressed class, its lack of self-confidence, its instinct for submission to the state. These parties have been passively dragged into the world catastrophe and making a cowardly virtue of necessity, took it upon themselves to cover-up an unprincipled bloody crime with the lie of liberation mythology. Arising from a half-century of world antagonisms the military catastrophe was a disaster transferred onto the edifice of the 50 year-old International. The anniversary of the war is also the anniversary of the most terrible fall of the strongest parties of the international proletariat.

And yet we meet the bloody anniversary without any mental decline or political skepticism. Revolutionary internationalists had the inestimable advantage that they held their position in the face of the world's greatest catastrophe, with analysis, criticism and revolutionary foresight. We renounced all the "national" point-scoring issuing from the General Staff, not only those with a cheap price tag, but even those with a surcharge. We continued to see things as they are, to call them by their names and anticipate the logic of their further movement. We have seen how, in a mad kaleidoscope in front of bleeding humanity, old illusions were adopted and new programmes hastily adapted to them, they were approved and, in the maelstrom of events, failed, yielding place to new illusions and more new programs that hurtled to the same fate, all the more exposing the truth. And the social truth is always revolutionary!

Marxism, the method of our orientation to the historical process and the instrument of our intervention in this process, is able to withstand the blows of 75 mm guns , as well as the 42 centimetre Mausers. It prevailed when the parties standing, it seemed, under its banner were shattered. Marxism is not a snap-shot of working class consciousness - it gives the laws of historical development of the working class. In its struggle for liberation the working class can be unfaithful to Marxism – by sheer force of circumstances, the analysis of which constitutes Marxism - but in betraying Marxism, the working class betrays itself. Through downfall and disappointment, through tragic disasters, arriving at new, higher forms of self-knowledge, the working class again comes to Marxism, consolidating and deepening in its consciousness its latest revolutionary conclusions.

This is the process that we have seen over the last year. The logic of the situation of the working class powerfully drives it out everywhere from under the yoke of the national bloc and - an even greater miracle! – clears out from many socialist brains the mould of possibilism. Despite their apparent success, how pathetic and contemptible seem the hasty efforts of the official parties once again to proclaim at their meetings, the revolutionary role of the states' melinite[4] and to inculcate, through multiple repetition, the slavish illusion of "the defense of the fatherland", not leaving the great imperialist road!

The hopeless military situation, the parasitic greed of the ruling capitalist cliques feeding on this hopelessness, the widespread growth of armed reaction, the impoverishment of the masses and as a result of this, a slow but steady sobering of the working class - this is a genuine reality, the further development of which will not be held back by any force in the world! In the bowels of all the parties of the International is a process, as yet only an ideological revolt, against militarism and chauvinist ideology - a process that not only saves the honor of socialism, but also indicates to the nations the only way out of the war, with its slogan "to the end", this finished formulation coming up against the blind alley of "scientific barbarism".

To serve this process is the highest task which now exists on our bloody and dishonored planet!

Notes

1. From *Nashe Slovo, (Our Word)*, 4th August 1915. First translation from Russian.
2. Quadruple Entente, or just Entente, referred to the alliance of Britain, France, Russia and Japan.
3. The seven powers were Germany, Britain, France, Russia, Austria-Hungary, Japan and Italy. The eighth referred to is the USA
4. A chemical used to make explosives.

The Military Disaster and Political Perspectives[1]

Square brackets [] indicate material removed by the censor. Where the text was re-inserted in later editions this is shown inside these brackets

I. The Causes of the Crisis

Now that the clearing out of Russian forces from Galicia, Poland and the Baltic region has become the largest established fact in the overall picture of the war, the censorship in the French Republic will perhaps give us the opportunity to dwell on the reasons. We note here, with no claim to having a gift of prophesy, that we had anticipated such an outcome at the time the French press was writing about the imminent entry of Russian Cossacks into Berlin. But we were forced to remain silent: the privilege of free expression is enjoyed only by those who do not anticipate anything and do not understand anything.

The Russian failure is explained by a lack of guns and ammunition. But where did this come from? They say that Russia, as well as its allies, were not prepared for an attack. But what was the Russian army of nearly half a million men there for? For the purposes of defence it is said. But why was it not possible to prepare for defence? We never for a moment doubt the evil intent of Germany. We just fail to see proof of the good intent of Suhomlinov's firm in the military failure.[2]

Hervé,[3] who has written with similar contempt about German "culture" and enthusiastically declared: "Long live the Tsar!", now claims that the German army has "huge material and moral superiority over Russia" That's more than a shortage of ammunition caused by the Minister of War's lack of foresight.

Germany's military successes are, in the final analysis, the result of a high level of capitalist organization. Military technique is just the application of general technique in the field of the mutual extermination of peoples. Indeed, military organization forms the point of least resistance in backward countries in the process of modernisation. All states, regardless of their economic level and national culture, strive to match up in advanced military technology. But the dependence of military equipment on the general level of society is always in the end decisive. It is not enough to have the latest design of guns - you need to be able to continuously update them, increase output and maximise their rate of fire.

German industry - especially heavy industry, which is crucial to militarism - due to its relatively recent origin is very rationalized, i.e. as free from the clutches of routine as is possible in a capitalist economy. It is precisely this that accounts for her performance. In this war, Germany represents a powerful *industrial* country compared to Russia, with its mainly *agricultural* population. Her industry is *large* and *centralised* compared to France, which is still dominated by *small* and *medium* industry. She has *modern* and *streamlined* management practices compared to the technically very *conservative* old capitalist power of England - for all its technical progress in recent years. Such is the economic foundation of the military power of Germany, which pulls behind her Austria and Turkey.

Russian heavy industry undeniably has a dominant place in the country's economic life. But safely protected behind tariff walls, not hesitating periodically to put the country on a starvation diet of coal and iron, carrying out the latest development in state policy, whose supreme ideal is "the nationalization of credit", accustomed to being fed with unlimited state orders, Russian heavy industry is saturated to the core with technical incompetence and economic parasitism. This alone, apart from anything else, precludes the possibility of any sudden and miraculous results from the so-called "industrial mobilization". No wonder Guchkov[4] who knows what's what, warned the military-industrial conference against undue optimism.

As people are the main force behind production, so it is with war. So how does the Russian army stand with its human material?

Plekhanov[5] wrote in his pamphlet on the war that the Russian army is made up of lions commanded ... not by lions. We are not in a position to say exactly who does "command", we will leave it to the quick-witted reader to complete the spirited quote. In what sense however should "lion" be understood, the Russian army consisting in the most part of peasants? Does this mean that the Russian *race* is superior in war-likeness to other peoples, or that the Russian peasant has been though a special historical school of heroism? Or, under the lion characterisation, Plekhanov has begun to understand the Russian peasants' enduring ability to meekly starve, rot and die? What meaning does the first half of the quote have? None. This is one of those meaningless platitudes that feed a terminally doomed social patriotism, especially in Russia.

Elementary Marxist thought suggests that the most important part of a modern army is the industrial proletariat. The more capitalist technique begins to play a role in the modern military, the greater the importance the worker-technician assumes. No matter how great the industrial, social and political importance of our working class, numerically it still represents a small fraction of the population, while remaining essentially deeply hostile to the goals under which it was mobilized by Tsarism. Conscription like universal suffrage automatically reflects the numerical ratio of social groupings in society. In the Russian army especially, the peasantry overwhelms the proletariat, numerous elements of the latter, the most qualified, are held in factories for industrial war service. Having an overwhelmingly peasant army cannot but lower its military level.

This circumstance is compounded by the historically conditioned character of the Russian peasantry. The smallholders of France, coming out of the Great Revolution, and taking possession of the lands of the monarchy and the nobility, then went through the school of compulsory education and the school of republican parliamentarism, and approached in this way the cultural level of the city. The Russian peasants, to this day still enmeshed in a system without any rights to their estate property, infinitely far from being able to feel themselves "owners of the land " - a title the Jordanskiis[6] dispense to all in military dress uniform – are neither master of the land or master of the state. The 1905 Revolution tried - and this experience has not gone away - to arouse the peasantry to a conscious and active historical life. The victorious counter-revolution for its part, tried - and with considerable success - to minimize the cultural fruits of the revolution in the life of the village. If, in the last decades, at least a certain quantitative progress in the field of national education has been made, those generations of the Russian village which now fill up the Russian army, in any event, did not have time to experience the new school system - but they were able to take part in punitive expeditions.[7]

After the Russian peasantry, tens of millions of ethnic national minorities need to be taken into account. However much the bourgeois representatives of the latter in the Duma testify to their patriotic enthusiasm, there is no doubt that the vile system of exceptional laws, supplemented by pogroms, is little able to feed the " leonine" patriotic sentiment of the national minority masses, who do not have the right of free expression or the right of residence in the very country they are called upon to defend.

What about those "non- lions" who *command* the Russian army? On this account, we will say only - and this will be enough - that the officer class, especially in the upper tier of the leadership, represent an inseparable part of the June 3rd rulers of Russia.[8] Here you find one uniform layer of people, methods and attitudes. Recruited from the same social circles, the senior officers and top bureaucrats are always just conduits, with the same cultural and moral level. No further explanation is required.

The reasons for the failure of the Russian army are deeper than a simple lack of shells in the warehouses of Suhomlinov. In 1890, Friedrich Engels wrote about Tsarist Russia: "Russia likes only those wars where its allies have to bear the main burden, to open their territory to devastation, to provide the bulk of the combatants and where the Russian troops are kept in reserve. Only against the very weakest, like Sweden, Turkey, or Persia, the Tsarist government wages war alone". In the quarter century that has passed since these words were written, the economic and social life of Russia has undergone enormous changes. These changes found their expression in the 1905 revolution. But Bourgeois France helped the tsarist government to cope with the revolution. The Russia of the 3rd of June remained a monarchy of bureaucratic caste bondage. On this basis, Russian imperialism grew and renewed Russian militarism. The events of the war exposed militarism to a decisive test. The results are available. The further course of military operations - in Russia, as well as on other fronts - can make very substantial changes to the situation, but in its basic features Russia's military role is determined. The suppressed revolution has taken revenge. An aggressive imperialism, uniting under its banner all the parties of the ruling classes and subjugating the political conscience of the Russian intelligentsia, sums up the story. From this point the further political development of the country will proceed.

II. Defeat and revolution

War is a historical examination of class society, verifying by force its material basis, the material linkages between classes, and the stability and flexibility of state organization. In this sense it is possible to say that *victory* - other things being equal - demonstrates the relative strength of a given state structure, increases its authority and thus strengthens it. On the other hand *defeat*, discredits the state organization, so weakening it.

Before the war, no sane social-democrat believed that Russia, having undergone a victorious counter-revolution, would be able to establish a victorious imperialism. No-one doubted that the war would open up all the existing cracks in society and in the state. At that time, our party was consistently against the war. It never occurred to us to link our political hopes, reformist or revolutionary, to Tsarism's military misfortunes, which seemed inevitable to us in case of war, beyond any doubt. This was not because we regarded it as "morally unacceptable" for the revolutionary class to be interested in the military collapse of its government, as do the social-patriotic sycophants today. Nor was it due to any blind nation-state instincts, which in Russian revolutionary circles are strongly counterbalanced by a sufficiently strong hatred of Tsarism. Nor, finally, was it due to any general humanitarian considerations regarding the disasters inevitably associated with war. The "normal" life of class society for centuries and millennia, has been built on the most horrific miseries of the masses - the war only concentrates in time these miseries. And if the surest and shortest way to emancipation lay through war, revolutionary Social-Democracy would not have hesitated to take it. The resolve of a surgeon is not undermined by the prospect of suffering and blood, when he considers that resorting to the knife is necessary.

If we refused to speculate on the war and the defeat it may bring, this was not for national or humanitarian reasons, but due to revolutionary political considerations, both international and internal.

A defeat, other things being equal, that shatters one state structure, implies the corresponding strengthening of that of its adversary. And we do not know of any social and state organisation in Europe, that it would be in the interests of the European proletariat to strengthen. At the same time, we do not in any sense allot to Russia, the role of the state whose interests must be subordinated to the interests of the development of other European nations. It is hardly necessary to dwell on this side of the question, which has been adequately clarified in the columns of our paper.

But even without departing from the framework of narrow national prospects for development, the Russian Social-Democracy could not link its political plans with the revolutionising influence of military disasters.

Defeats can serve as the indisputable and indispensable driving force of development only under certain historical circumstances, when the necessity for internal transformation has matured and is not matched by the presence in the bowels of society of new historical classes capable of implementing or forcing the transformation. In such circumstances, the reforms carried out from above, as a result of defeat, can give a major impetus to the development of progressive social classes. But war is too contradictory and double-edged a factor in historical development for a revolutionary party, that feels a firm class foundation under its feet and is confident of its future, to see the road of defeat as the road to political success.

Defeat disorganises and demoralises the ruling reaction, but at the same time the war disorganises the whole of social life, especially the working class.

War is not an "auxiliary" factor, over which the revolutionary class can have control. It cannot be removed at will after giving the revolutionary impetus expected of it, like some historical Moor,[9] who has completed his job.

Finally, having grown out of defeats, a revolution inherits an economic life completely disordered by war, depleted public finances and very strained international relations.

If for Russian Social Democracy, adventurist speculation remained quite foreign, even in the darkest years of the triumph of the counter-revolution, this was because war, while it may give an impetus to revolution, can at the same time create an environment that will make the social and political use of a revolutionary victory very difficult.

However, we have now not only to *assess* in which direction war and defeat affect the course of political development, we have above all to *act* on the terrain that the defeat actually creates. For whatever the further vicissitudes of military events - one can say with absolute certainty: there is no serious possibility of Russia restoring and increasing her power quickly enough to still be able to achieve her plans for world conquest in the present war. The tsarist army has been defeated. It may have some successes, but it has lost the war. The recent defeats mark the beginning of a military catastrophe.

Again we must repeat: Social Democracy does not create arbitrarily the historical situation in which it operates. It represents only one of the forces in the historical process. It must operate on the terrain created for it by history.

The present generation of leaders of all the political parties in Russia, has been brought up entirely on the experience of the last 10 - 15 years in the development of our country. For this reason alone, to think about the possible consequences of internal military disaster inevitably suggests an analogy with the events of 1903 – 1905. In 1903, a violent wave of mass strikes shook Russia. Social Democracy saw in these events a prologue to revolution. In January 1904 the Russo-Japanese war began. It immediately stopped the revolutionary movement. This lasted more than six months as if the country had frozen. Losses in the war theatre demoralized and weakened state power and gave a powerful impetus to the discontent of different social classes and groups. On this basis, the revolution made feverish progress.

The years 1912-1913, as in 1903, saw a picture of a growing mass movement, again mainly in the form of revolutionary proletarian strikes. The Labour Movement was now developing at an incomparably higher level, drawing on the experience of the most stormy and meaningful decade in the history of Russia. Like before, the outbreak of war immediately suspended the development of the revolutionary movement. Almost complete silence descended on the country. The State, after the first victories, which had a totally contingent nature, completely lost its head and took a reactionary course, that pre-revolutionary Russia had not known. But the period of "victories" quickly came to an end. The subsequent continuous defeats [finally brought down the ruling clique, provoked the patriotic indignation of the bourgeois-landlord block and so] created more favourable external conditions for the development of a broad social movement. By analogy with the last decade, we can surmise that after the "opposition" mobilisation of the propertied classes, there must follow the mobilisation of the democracy, and at its head, the proletariat, resulting in revolutionary upheavals.

It is highly significant that hopes in the salutary and liberating role of Russian defeats began to be spread by those who most ardently wished for Russian victories. British Minister Lloyd George has already seen the Russian giant, awakened by disaster, throwing off the shackles of the reaction. Vandervelde,[10] who at the beginning of the war was persuading our Duma faction of the progressive value of future Russian victories, now authoritatively moralises about the salutariness of Russian defeats. Hervé writes about the beneficence of suffering as a factor in Russian history. Finally, some social-patriotic turn-coats, reasoning in the months of Russian successes with the formula: "first victory, then reform", have begun to bustle about an amnesty ... after the purging of Warsaw. In this explicit "defeatism" there is of course, no revolutionary element. Lloyd George, Vandervelde and Herve - they simply hope that the military defeat will awaken "the public mind" of the ruling classes of Russia. With a deep inner contempt for Russia, all of them in relation to this are *naked* defeatists, relying on the independent automatic impact of a military collapse - without the direct intervention of the revolutionary classes. Meanwhile, from our point of view, central to the immediate fate of Russia is the question of the impact of war and defeat on the awakening, cohesion and activity of the revolutionary forces.

From this perspective, it is necessary above all to say that it would be a severe mistake to simply transfer to the present epoch past experience in relation to the impact of war on the mood of the masses. The current catastrophe is on a giant scale, and consequently, in its disruptive effects on the economic and cultural life of the country, cannot be compared with the colonial adventure of the Russo-Japanese war. On the other hand, the effect of the present defeat should, of course, lead to a much broader and deeper impact on the consciousness of the working masses. The Social Democrats are now finding inexhaustible sources for revolutionary agitation, every word of which will be met with a powerful resonance. But it is necessary on the other hand, to take clearly into account that military catastrophe, depleting as it does the economic and spiritual forces and resources of the population, retains a capacity only within certain *limits* to induce active anger, protest and revolutionary action. Beyond a certain point, exhaustion can be so great as to suppress energy and paralyse the will. Hopelessness, passivity and moral decay begins. [The link between defeat and revolution does not have a mechanical, but dialectical character].

The hopes of Lloyd-George and others that the pressure of defeats alone will be sufficient to "enlighten" Russia's rulers towards liberalism, only reflects the latter's hopeless vulgarity. On the other hand, it would be a childish delusion to conclude, on the basis of an incorrect interpretation of the "Russo-Japanese" experience, that military defeats automatically have a revolutionary impact on the masses. Just the huge dimensions of the current war – with its *indefinitely prolonged character* – may for a long time hamstring all social development and, therefore, in the first place, the revolutionary movement of the proletariat.

[Hence the need to struggle for a speedy end to the war. The revolution is not interested in a further accumulation of defeats. The struggle for peace is for us dictated by revolutionary self-preservation. The more powerfully the toiling masses are mobilized against the war, the more fully will the experience of defeat provide a political lesson for the working class, and the sooner it will be transformed into a force stimulating the revolutionary movement].

Notes

1. First published in *Nashe Slovo, (Our Word),* August 26, 1, 2 September 1915. First full translation into English. This article comprises the first two parts of a four part series. Part 3, 'Social Forces of the Revolution' was published on 3rd September, and Part 4, 'A National or International Course' on 4th September.
2. V A Sukhomlinov. Russian Minister of War until July 1915.
3. Gustave Hervé, founder of the paper *La Guerre Sociale*. Took a left pacifist position before the war, but quickly moved to ultra-nationalism after July 1914.
4. Alexander Guchkov, leader of the pro-war Octobrist Party in Russia. Earlier had been head of the Committee for National Defense for five years.
5. Georgi Plekhanov. Founder of Russian Marxism but supported the war, leading to Lenin calling him a social chauvinist.
6. This is a somewhat obscure reference to N Jordansky, at the time a follower of Plekhanov. He gives his name in the plural presumably to include Plekhanov. Trotsky had just written an attack on Jordansky ('Out of Order', *Nashe Slovo*, 15th August 1915) for his defence of the custom of students and officials under Tsarism to wear military uniforms.
7. A reference to pogroms against the Jews
8. The June 3rd rulers of Russia refers to the regime that came to power after the suppression of the 2nd Duma, a result of the 1905 revolution, on 3rd June 1907.
9. The Moor refers to a character in Schiller's 'The Robbers', who after having carried out an unpleasant task for the King, is summarily dismissed.
10. Emile Vandervelde, Belgian socialist who joined his government on the outbreak of war and appealed to the Social Democrats in Russia to back the Tsarist regime.

The National Principle[1]

Almost no news has penetrated the French press about the recent Lausanne Congress of Small and Oppressed Nationalities. If you consider that the Allies are fighting for "the national principle"- in case they had forgotten, Mr Sazonov[2] again reminded the Americans about it - at first sight such inattention to the Lausanne Congress could get confusing. But actually ... it is very clear.

Those, however, who still persist in their misunderstanding, should poke their noses in the new issue of *L'Eclair*. This strange newspaper, combining attention to the celestial dogma of Catholicism with the progressive aspirations of French industry - neither are platonic - gives space from time to time to reports and articles, where, to a significant extent, an element of genuine truth sticks out.

First of all it turned out - what a surprise for Plekhanov[3] who lives near Lausanne! - that at the Congress of Oppressed People "among the twenty three nationalities were representatives almost all the national minorities of Russia: Finns, Lithuanians, Latvians, Poles, Ukrainians, Georgians, etc, etc," (the author, obviously from Allied tact, breaks off the list here). There were also representatives of the Irish people, Albanians, Egyptians and Tunisians. There was even Mr Aberson, representing the Jews as a nationality.

Concerning the Congress resolutions recognizing each nation's right to self-determination, *L'Eclair* candidly observes:

"The difficulty in the practical implementation of this programme is that everyone readily acknowledges the freedom of their enemies' national minorities, but not their own or those of their allies".

"In the Allied camp for example, they demand the freedom of non-German nationalities, subjugated by Germany and Austria, and non-Turkish ethnic groups, subjugated by Turkey, but would like to give Russia the opportunity to exercise discretion regarding her minorities".

Even in the atmosphere of the obligatory lie we have been breathing for two years, these are not, God knows, new or daring thoughts, revealed in a "big" French newspaper, in some way refreshing to the soul. And to think that there are Russian *socialists*, Russian *revolutionaries*, Russian *migrants*, who before the Congress in Lausanne, where the Kyrgyz came to complain about the Tsarist yoke, continue to join in the chorus of Mr Sazonov about the liberation objectives pursued in this war by Russia. No one demands of these people internationalism, but if they were just honest *patriotic democrats*, they would burn with shame!

However, to avoid embarrassment they always have in reserve a reference to the Allies: Russia, of course, is an oppressive country, but with the help of the "Western democracies" it will - through victory - deliver all the internal and external miracles that Germany must come to, through defeat.

How really are things with the Allies on this issue? Leave alone for now the Far East, where Russia, in alliance with Japan, is going to implement in the coming decades "the national principle" on the back of China. It will be time to think about the half-billion Chinese, when Plekhanov and Kuropatkin call for the freedom of Schleswig-Holstein![4] Let us confine ourselves to the "Western democracies". But we will not raise the Irish question, because it is well-known how magnanimously Britain is implementing home rule in Dublin. However, Connolly and the other rebels who have been hanged or shot will not be able to enjoy an Irish Parliament, since they themselves are now being enjoyed by a parliament of worms underground. But let's leave Ireland. Let's leave Britain entirely. What is the situation in France?

For the colonial powers like France or England, says *L'Eclair*, the question of the "natives", which was looked into at Lausanne, is of particular interest. The Lausanne Conference resolution does not want to recognise the separation of the races into "lower" and "higher", since this is the philosophy of colonial domination, that in general they rely on most. *L'Eclair*, on this account, calls for colonial "democracy", justice and ... caution, at the same time noting with satisfaction, the moving of a bill during the Lausanne Conference by Deputy Doazi, by which Algerians would be given "serious" representation in the institutions that discuss their interests. This is very comforting. But the fact is that at the same time, i.e. almost during the sessions of the Lausanne Congress, in the Far East, in French Indo-China, an event took place significantly less favourable from the point of view of the "national principle". In Annam [Translator's note: part of present day Vietnam], which was set up in 1884 as a French protectorate, i.e. actually a French colony, an uprising took place under the banner of national independence. The French press was allowed to write about it for a few weeks after the event, but the patriotic and right-thinking papers did not avail themselves of the opportunity. Of course, *L'Humanité*[5] - this organ of bigotry, hypocrisy and lies, did not even hint at an event vitally linked to the destiny of five and a half million Annamites. And if we have now a "censorship beating opportunity" to give readers information, albeit scant, about the Annamite rebellion, then it is again thanks to the same reactionary organ *L'Eclair*.

The young Emperor of Annam, Duy Tan, who was essentially only a native-royalist ornament fronting colonial domination of the Republic, entered into communication with a national revolutionary organization of his subjects. By agreement with them, he escaped from his palace to the country, and addressed the nation with a revolutionary appeal, declaring the independence of Annam. But the government of the Third Republic turned out to be master of the situation. The rebel was caught, brought back to "their" capital of Hué, deposed and locked up in a fortress, where he now has enough leisure time, not only to learn by heart the Declaration of Rights, but also to read the full set of *L'Humanité* for the duration of the war (if, of course, the deposed Emperor is allowed to read newspapers in prison).

In these far-off countries - we take a sample quote from *Revue Hebdomadaire,*[6] to show the distance between reality and official ideology - "in these distant countries, the soul of the people trembles as one with the soul of the French people, in the Far East, which seemed (!) almost hostile to us, we see a moving picture of how thousands of priests offer prayers to Buddha for the victory of our arms", etc. etc. This was written in the autumn of last year ... But in approximately a month, when the Far Eastern "Emperor"- who was recently organising preparations for the day of the '75' gun,[7] this was written about with emotion as well- will be eating his prison rations for the 30th day; in France they will have forgotten about the rebellion and the few who know about it, - the patriotic and social-patriotic scribblers, will again begin to write emotionally about the "trembling" Annamite soul. Not only that. Every time the Indochinese soldiers who have been brought here catch the eye of Renaudel, he will remind the workers of France that the Republic incorporates their lesser Annamite brothers in the great struggle for the "national principle".

Paris.

Notes

1. Published in *Nashe Slovo, (Our Word),* July 13, 1916. First translation into English.
2. S D Sazonov, (1860-1927) Russian Foreign Minister until July 1916.
3. G Plekhanov. Founder of Russian Marxism. In WW1, took a nationalist, pro-war position, leading to Lenin calling him a Social Chauvinist.
4. A N Kuropatkin (1848-1925), former minister in Imperial Russia, was appointed Commander in Chief of the Russian northern armies in February 1916. Schleswig-Holstein is a disputed region on the borders of Denmark and Germany.
5. *L'Humanité* was a pro-war daily socialist paper, edited by Pierre Renaudel from 1914-18. It subsequently became the organ of the French Communist Party.

6. Right-wing French weekly paper.
7. Day of the "75" gun is probably a reference to the battle of the Somme. The 75mm gun was the mainstay of the Allied artillery, in which great but unfounded hope was placed to destroy German defensive positions before the battle began.

Serb Terrorists and French 'Liberators'. The Mood in Vienna in the First Days of the War[1]

A direct impetus to the immeasurable events of the present war was given by a few Serb youths, almost boys, who killed the heir to the Austro-Hungarian throne in July 1914 in Sarajevo. National romantic-revolutionaries, they, least of all, expected the global consequences of what unfolded from their terrorist act. I later met a member of this revolutionary organization in Paris, in the first months of the war. He belonged to the group that organised the assassination of Archduke Franz Ferdinand, but he went abroad before the murder, and in the first days of the war joined as a volunteer in the French navy as a translator. At that time, the allies organised a landing on the Adriatic coast of Austro-Hungary in Dalmatia,[2] having the intention to support an uprising in the South-Slav provinces of the Habsburg monarchy. For this purpose the French war ships stocked a Serbian press to print revolutionary proclamations and enrolled dedicated young Serbs who were to make these appeals and generally raise a rebellion for "national independence". Officially they were known as translators. Since, however, the Serbian revolutionaries on the warships of the Republic were made of far too combustible material, a silver-haired Serb spy was placed on the flag ship for "internal" surveillance of the young enthusiasts. It is very likely that this wise foresight should to be attributed to the Russian Embassy in Paris, which in general in all such operations has uncontested hegemony (leadership) among the allies.

The entire enterprise, as we know, came to nothing. The French ships circled in the Adriatic, came up to Pula, but after several inconclusive volleys returned home. -Why? –asked the uninitiated with bewilderment. But in French journalistic and political circles the explanation had already been given in private: "Italy is against it". An uprising in the southern provinces of Austria-Hungary could clearly only be under the banner of the national unification of the South Slavs. Meanwhile, Italy considered that Dalmatia should belong to her "as of right" - obviously, by the right of her imperialist appetite - and she lodged a protest against the expected allied landings. At that time it was necessary to pay a price for the benevolent neutrality of Italy, as for its later intervention in the war: that's why the French ships so unexpectedly turned back with their press, Serbs-translators and silver haired Sleuth.

"How do you explain this, the young Serbian revolutionary, who I mentioned above, asks me? -It turns out that the allies, without ceremony, are simply selling the Serbs to Italy. Where is the war for the liberation of small nations now? And in that case, what are we, the Serbs, dying for? I didn't volunteer only to facilitate, with my blood, the transition of Dalmatia to Italy? And in the name of what did my friend in Sarajevo, Gavrilo Princip[3] and others perish?"

He was in despair, the young man with a dark, slightly pock-marked face and feverishly glittering eyes. The true background of the war of "liberation" was revealed to them from its Dalmatian angle ... From him I learned many details about the internal life of the South-Slav revolutionary organizations and, in particular, about the group of boys who killed the heir to the Habsburg throne, the head of the Austro-Hungarian military party.

The organization, with the romantic name "Crna Ruka" ("the Black Hand"), was built on strictly-conspiratorial carbonari [Translator's note: The Carbonari were Italian revolutionaries who fought in the 19th Century against Austrian rule] principles. The new members went through mysterious rituals: a knife was put to the bared chest, an oath of silence and loyalty was taken on pain of death, etc. The strands of this organization, which had branches in all the South-Slav provinces of the Habsburg monarchy and was filled with self-sacrificing students, were gathered in Belgrade, in the hands of officers and politicians equally close to the Serbian Government and to the Russian Embassy. Agents of the Romanovs in the Balkans, as is well known, have never stopped using dynamite.

That Vienna was dressed in official mourning did not prevent the masses of the urban poor being quite indifferent to the news of the death of the heir to the Habsburg throne. But immediately the press got to work on public opinion. In the events of the present war, it's hard to find sufficiently graphic words to describe the truly villainous role played by the press all over Europe and around the world. In this orgy of baseness, the Austro-Hungarian black and yellow press, not over-blessed with knowledge or talent, indisputably occupies not the last place. Since the assassination in Sarajevo, on a command from the unseen Center - the diplomatic cauldron, where the destiny of peoples is decided - hacks of all political shades mobilized as many lies as has been seen since the creation of the world.

We, the socialists, with quiet contempt, could see in the Cain-like work of the "patriotic" press on both sides of the trenches, irresistible proof of the moral decadence of bourgeois society, if ... if only the prominent socialist organs had not followed the same path. That's what was doubly terrible to us, because it was an unexpected blow. However, as far as the Vienna "Arbeiter Zeitung" ("Workers Paper"), is concerned it was only half-unexpected. In the seven years of my life in Vienna (1907-1914), I got close enough to get acquainted with the mindset of the leadership of the Austrian Social Democracy and least of all expected any revolutionary initiative from its side. The purely chauvinistic character of the articles of Leitner, Foreign Editor at the paper, was already sufficiently known before the war. Back in 1909, I had to speak out in *Neue Zeit*[4] against the Prussian-Austrian line of the central organ of the Austrian Social Democracy. During trips to the Balkans I have often heard from the people there, especially from Serb socialists (particularly from my unforgettable friend Dmitry Tucoviča killed, serving as an officer, during the war) indignant complaints that the Serbian bourgeois press all gloatingly quoted the chauvinistic rhetoric of the "Arbeiter Zeitung" against the Serbs, as proof that international solidarity of workers is only a fairy-tail. Despite all this, I did not expect from the "Arbeiter Zeitung" the unbridled misanthropy of this newspaper in the first period of the war.

After Austro-Hungary's well known ultimatum to Serbia a patriotic demonstration began in Vienna. The participants were predominantly teenagers. There was not real chauvinism in the crowd, but excitement and infatuation, waiting for some great events and changes, for the better of course, because nothing could get worse... And the press frenziedly exploited this mood, worked it up and aggravated it.

"Everything now depends on the behaviour of Russia, a socialist member of the Reichstag, Leopold Winarski, who died last year, told me - if the Tsar intervenes, the war will become popular here".

And really, there is no doubt that the spectre of a tsarist invasion of Austria and Germany extraordinarily agitated the imagination of the Austro-German masses. The international reputation of the tsarist regime, especially in the epoch after the counterrevolution,[5] had a very definite character and it's possible to say led the Austro-German politicians and journalists to declare war against eastern "liberation" despotism. This does not justify in the slightest, of course, the Scheidemans,[6] who immediately started the translation of Hohenzollern lies into "socialist" language. But it reveals to us the whole of the abyss that our Plekhanov and Deutsch[7] fell into, who in their declining days, discovered their vocation as advocates of tsarist diplomacy in the era of its greatest crimes.

Notes

1. Written in 1916. First published in *Kommunist* 151, Petrograd, 1919. First translation into English
2. Dalmatia is part of present day Croatia

3. Gavrilo Princip (1894-1918) Assassin of Arch-Duke Franz Ferdinand. In fact, Princip was still alive at the time Trotsky spoke to his informant.
4. *Die Neue Zeit* - the theoretical organ of the German Social Democratic Party
5. 'Counterrevolution' is a reference to the reaction that followed the defeat of the Russian Revolution of 1905.
6 Philipp Scheidemann (1865-1939). Right wing leader of German Social Democratic Party. Responsible for the murder of Rosa Luxemburg and Karl Leibnicht.
7. G V Plekhanov (1856-1918) and L G Deutsch (1855-1941). Founders of Russian Marxism.

War Correspondence

'Guerre D'Usure'[1]

[Translator's note: *'Guerre D'Usure'* means 'War of Attrition']

In none of theatres of war has either side achieved decisive results. As yet there are no winners and no losers, except for military routine. But the collapse of the latter sticks out with such clarity that only military-Bourbons can deny it, those, who, like the Bourbons in the France of old, forget nothing and learn nothing.

The conviction that the army consists of its regulars, and the rest of the mass of the adult male population is only raw or semi-finished material, playing a secondary role as reserves, a belief representing a compromise between the idea of a professional army of the old type and the principle of universal military service, turned out to be fundamentally untenable. It is precisely the so-called reserves that make up the real functioning army, that decides the fate, not of skirmishes and battles, but of wars and countries.

German strategy, combining feudal methods of thought with capitalist resources, was built on the plan of the rapid onslaught, an overwhelming first-strike force. Subordinated to this plan was the entire organization of the German army - the most perfect of its kind. In the first weeks of the war, it seemed that this strategy was vindicated. But a modern great nation, with its huge resources, with its multi-million population, intelligent and full of initiative, cannot be forced to surrender by the onslaught of a few hundred thousand well-armed men. Under the most terrible blows, the country attacked always finds a way to gather together its main forces and reserves, and the more the attacker moves the centre of gravity onto the offensive at any cost, the more quickly will it be wiped out in the first battles of the regular forces - long before it comes to decisive military developments. The collapse of the German plan against France - to seize it in a few weeks, or a month or two, with the combined forces of a human avalanche, mausers, armoured cars and zepplins - was the collapse of routinist military planning, even with the world's best instruments of annihilation.

If nevertheless, Germany took over the most industrial and wealthy provinces of France, it is because French routine came to the assistance of German military routine. Up against the basic conditions of its existence: a relatively small population, economic stagnation and democratic forms of government, the Third Republic[2] was stretched to the limit in matching its regular soldiers with those of Germany. It could only achieve this at the expense of the equipment of the reserves. The more a great part of military trained young men are retained under the colours, and the longer they are held there, the less there is to spend on training and full equipment for the reserves. This discrepancy between the character of the French army and the social conditions of the French nation, was so disastrously revealed in the first period of the campaign. Impatiently demanding that Britain should move its makeshift army across the channel as soon as possible, and annoyed at her excessive orderliness, the French military and politicians thereby completely condemn their latest counter-reform, a return to a three-year period of military service and the organizing principle itself. In this the army sees its strength in its regular cadre, while in essence they serve only as a military school, the real army is completely dissolved into the reserves when tested. "At the present time, says one military writer - Germany is (on the question of regular and newly created armed forces) in the same position as England. Germany also cannot increase its combat ranks except by armies, intelligently organized anew. The advantages it derived from its very strong peacetime organization disappeared, and now it is not necessary to ask what worth can be given to the regular soldiers, because improvisation is now the rule everywhere - we need to ask, what worth can be given to the people, as individuals". In other words: the further course of the battles will not even to a small extent be determined by the barracks of peacetime, but by the general level of development of the human material from which new units are now being built.

The strategy of the rapid onslaught, designed mainly for regular troops, quickly exhausted itself without decisive results. After the initial movement and battles, both sides established fixed positions. To escape the destructive power of the shells, both armies buried themselves in the ground. In particular, the French managed to close up the most gaping holes in its military training. *Guerre d'usure* took the place of *'attaque brusquee'*, in place of the rapid *onslaught* - a strategy of *attrition*.

This definition, guerre d'usure, close fitting the Russian expression for "attrition", was at one time a very popular answer to the question of what will happen next. When it was said that the Germans would be starved out, this was well understood. This included not only the gradual collapse of the German army, but, above all, the economic collapse of the country. Reality brought cruel disappointment. Firstly, people remembered that Germany is third in the world in agricultural output. Secondly, that trade in wartime as in peacetime, is not determined by diplomats or by national sympathies, but by the maximum profit. Exports of the United States to Europe and figures for the transit trade of Scandinavian countries, Italy and Switzerland prove it best. Finally, the note of the government of Woodrow Wilson[3] has destroyed the illusion of the possibility of a real trade blockade of Germany and Austria. It remains purely a war of military attrition. But as Clemenceau[4] wrote: "we would simply have been children to have thought that we could cling forever to this so-called guerre d'usure, which depletes us simultaneously with the enemy." You cannot for a moment forget that the brunt of military operations on the Western Front now lies entirely on the French army. The Belgians, who took the first blows, suffered terrible damage early in the campaign. After the capture of Namur and Liege, they were involved in the tragic retreat from Charleroi and participated in the battle of the Marne. Together with the remnants of the Antwerp garrison, the Belgian field army was severely damaged in the Flanders battles. Now the remnants have taken positions on the left flank, on the small part of the Belgian coast not captured by the Germans. According to local information, confirmed in the Swiss press, the Belgian army currently has no more than 30 thousand men. The conventional view of the British Expeditionary Force is also extremely exaggerated. The army of General French,[5] I have been personally informed, hardly reaches a quarter of a million, or rather, more truly, does not exceed 200,000. Its strength lies in the constant flow of reinforcements, which maintains its strength and morale. In addition, about 30 thousand Indians need to be added to the British total. A new Indian detachment recently arrived in Marseille. In any case, British and Belgian forces constitute no more than a sixth of the entire federal army under the high command of Joffre.

What are the further possibilities and perspectives?

Joffre's December endeavour, made apparently under political pressure, possibly it is said, in connection with the impending opening of Parliament, was an attempt to go onto the offensive along the whole line. This led to such modest success that you cannot even point to it with your fingernail on a wall map. The general offensive came down in practice to an increased probing along the entire front, sinking now, especially in Flanders, into the thick mud. On the other hand, all of the information available here about the German preparatory operations, demonstrates that the adversary sees himself forced to be limited in the coming winter months to purely defensive actions, concentrating his forces for a new decisive spring offensive, apparently chiefly on Dunkirk and the Pas-de-Calais. In any case, the forces of both armies are now so fixed, contact between them is so continuous, reconnaissance so versatile and broad that there is no reason to expect any sudden developments.

In truth, there is another factor of overriding importance that does not lend itself to prior accounting: the moral factor, the mood of the soldiers in both lines of trenches. In relation to this the Swiss Colonel Feiler, one of the most serious of the war critics, wrote: "often an offensive, which is the external means of victory, turns out only to be its confirmation. The battle, by means of its destructive power, has already achieved a victory. It demoralized the enemy, i.e. broke his nerve. However, the enemy still remains in place. The offensive forces him to take stock, which, in a state of demoralization, could only mean flight and surrender. Restoring morale in such a situation is possible only by bringing up fresh troops, i.e. those with nerves in one piece. Trench warfare has largely made it difficult to assess the degree of demoralization of the enemy and to make a preliminary estimate of his possible reactions. The reason is simple. Flight of the demoralized is not possible: it is almost tantamount to death because of the need to jump out of the trench in sight of the enemy, before starting to take to ones heels. But they run away precisely in order to avoid death. If flight increases the risk, it becomes a bad gamble. They must remain in the trench. Surrender then becomes the main reaction of the demoralized. But since demoralisation manifests itself as sluggish inactivity, the attacker has to go to the edge of the trench, at the risk of falling into it, to bring about or simply to verify the desired reaction. Clearly today it is more difficult to win a victory, or more precisely to verify it. In the past, during fine attacks across more or less open fields, a long line of infantry, numerous and united in a joint effort, with their reserves following behind, ready to replace them in the general charge, with one look frightened an already trembling enemy, seized by the impression of an uncontrollable onslaught. They didn't wait for the end. After one hundred or two hundred meters, they abandoned their position, revealing to those approaching a victory already gained. The initial attritional struggle prepared the ground for this. Demoralization immediately gripped the soul. The attack was only the final straw. There is nothing similar in relation to the trenches. For one or two hundred meters, there is no external indication to reveal the truth. The artillery is not as lively as usual? The slackening of the firing can be a trap. What's going on? Is it possible to hope for a victory? Do you need to fear a counterattack? Will the reaction show itself in the form of demoralization or inertia? Will some not put up any resistance? The trench remains a mystery. To reveal it, you need to get closer to the trench with a grenade in hand and a bayonet fixed to the gun-barrel ".

These striking lines were written shortly before the attempt of Joffre to go onto a general offensive (17 December 1914). This empirical testing of the psychological considerations of Feiler has shown that an authoritative military writer either overestimated the degree of decomposition already reached in the German trenches, or underestimated the fatigue in the French trenches. It is a fact that the spirit of self-confidence and belief in the rapid offensive that gripped the German army before the battle of the Marne and even before the battle of the Ijzer, now has disappeared. But this result was paid for at the expense of a deep weariness of the French army. *Guerre d'usure* exhausts both sides.

A front stretching for 400 kilometres from the sea to the Swiss frontier, gives a picture of the equilibrium of forces, already incapable of decisive initiative, but prepared, with the strength given by being dug-in, to defend their positions. By spring, the two armies will be further depleted - just one continuous bombardment by artillery is extremely destructive to the nerves! Only fresh forces could disrupt the settled balance. It is not about those reserves that are filling the open breaches in the army, it is about the new, freshly raised armies that must tip the balance in the spring.

What resources are there in Germany that are not yet exhausted?

Of course, the calculations of Colonel Repington, the military specialist of *The Times*, have been reported, who came to the pessimistic conclusion that the enemy can produce another 4 million fresh soldiers, including about 2 million aged 20 years and below and 2 million from the *Landwehr*[6] and *Landsturm*.[7] These alarming numbers, reproduced by the entire press, struck French public opinion very powerfully. In the last few days refutations have begun to appear. The first came from Colonel Feiler: he reduced Repington's figure by a million. The military critic of *L'Information*[8] wrote an article under the heading: "Germany has no more reserves." Based on the most general statistical calculations from the raw data on population, the author finds little that is well-founded that could put German strength at the beginning of the war at 6.404 million. Of this number, 2 million are completely out of action, on the Eastern front there are 1.5 million, and in the West -1.8 million, on their own territory (fortress garrisons etc.), there are at least 700 thousand souls. Together this gives six million. Therefore, Germany now has no more than 400 thousand fresh troops, aged 20-45 years old at its disposal. Colonel Rousset, introduced in the calculation of a coefficient of mistrust. He refuses to name even approximate figures due to the lack of any reliable data, but thinks that the Germans "have not yet exhausted all of their reserves".

There is no doubt, on the other side, General Joffre has far from exhausted all the human reserves of the country. There is widespread testing of men aged 25 to 47 years old, who were formerly released from service or posted to the rear. These tests are accompanied by a vigorous hunt for so-called 'embusques', i.e. draft dodgers. The patriotic press takes an active part in this hunt with Clemenceau at the head. The Test Commission, consisting everywhere of non-local doctors, massively lowered the criterion of fitness and energetically replenishes the ranks of the new army. In relation to the youth to be called up in 1915 and 1916, some newspapers, in particular the *Guerre Sociale*,[9] are agitating for the call-up of the next age category, i.e. boys of 17. They are also talking of an increase in the military age limit from 47 to 55 years. Several central stations serve as reception and distribution centres for the new army, they are remote enough from the front not to be at risk, and at the same time close enough to make possible the quick transfer of fresh forces. According to some calculations, which I won't begin to cite, and that could have, of course, only an approximate character, this second army will by the end of March include about a million soldiers, in any case unlikely to be more than 1.2 million. Different industries work day and night to prepare the necessary equipment for them. This task is more difficult since the northern industrial centres like Roubaix, are in the hands of the enemy. Special efforts are being made to create more heavy artillery, in which the main type is the medium gun, between 75 mm and the "Rimalo". In this way, the war Ministry is energetically forming a second, entirely new army, which in April will be thrown at the enemy positions.

We have seen how difficult it is to the uninitiated, i.e. to all but the General Staffs, to operate with the statistics in this area. But you can't give up on them, if you want to have at least a general idea of the balance of forces. Let's take the most likely figure for Germany, Feiler's 3 million. We will assume that only half of them will be sent to the Western theatre. The French army will be able to counter with a fresh army of nearly a million. The British promise to deliver Kitchener's[10] first army in the spring of 500 thousand men, of which the first 200 thousand are expected, but not before March. Thus the forces on both sides will be approximately equal. They must meet not in fresh positions, but in the old ones, along the length and breadth of the front. Major-General Gatti, military critic of the *Corriere della Sera*, thinks that the new clash, enriched with the experience of the previous months of war, and where the latest forces will be deployed, will be unusually concentrated in its cruelty and surpass everything we've seen so far. This is quite likely. Nevertheless, there can be no reason to think that the new second armies, on either side, will manage to decisively disturb the balance of forces and knock out the enemy from established positions. The trenches will be infused with fresh blood, but the war will continue as it is now: a guerre d'usure. And this is the most frightening prospect for France and is forcing her political ideas to be tossed in all directions.

Paris, January 15, 1915

Notes

1. Published in *Nashe Slovo, (Our Word),* 9th April 1915. First translation from Russian into any language.
2. The Third Republic was established in France after the Paris Commune in 1871 and lasted until the Second World War.
3. Woodrow Wilson was US President during WW1.
4. Georges Clemenceau was the leading bourgeois politician of the Third Republic. Initially refused to serve in government during the war, eventually became Prime Minister in 1917
5. Sir John French, Commander in Chief of the British Expeditionary Force for the first two years of the war.
6. *Landwehr* was the name given to the German reserve army. First raised in 1813.
7. *Landsturm* was the name given to the German and Austrian conscript armies.
8. *L'Information* - a French Republican paper, read in financial and industrial circles.
9. *La Guerre Sociale* - French Socialist newspaper founded by Gustave Hervé. Was anti-war until 29th July 1914. Subsequently took extreme social chauvinist position.
10. Lord Kitchener was British War Minister from 1914-16.

The 7th Infantry in the Belgian Epic[1]

I

In Leuven, as in the whole of Belgium, they did not believe the war until the last moment, they did not want to believe it, even at the last moment. They did not entirely believe it when German troops crossed the border. Belgians are a peaceful people, with a touch of the devil may care, transitional types between the French and the English: *on ne se fait beaucoup de bile* (they don't get upset easily). And when the first farm was set ablaze, the people still hoped that it was a misunderstanding. ...

Leuven - the quietest small town, personifying Belgium, in particular the old Belgium - with its petit-bourgeois civility and clericalism; in its provincialism, remote from the broad paths of world politics. At the heart of the life of the now devastated town stood the university, with its three to four thousand students. Future lawyers, doctors and prelates flooded the central streets and cafes. Piety did not prevent them having a good time. After their sprees, the students walked away with matchboxes, ashtrays, cups and even beer mugs in their pockets. This was the traditional, highly developed system of student requisitions that the Leuven publicans were forced to adapt to in their commercial calculations. The self-respecting students of Leuven are as proud of their confiscated ashtrays, as German student fraternities are of their duelling scars. In the summer, during the vacation, the town came completely to a standstill.

Belgian students enjoy exceptional privileges in relation to military service. There was a special student battalion in Leuven. The young people spent the night in the barracks, and as students spent the days in the classrooms and anatomy rooms. Among them was our friend Dennis De Baer, who had moved here from Brussels. His father, a strict conservative Catholic has - or, perhaps, you can say had - a covered vineyard near Brussels, three or four hectares, on which he grew dessert grapes of exceptional size and equally exceptional prices. The grapes were eaten mostly in Britain. The young De Baer was a lawyer, who worked with average necessary diligence, his studies were nearing their end, as was his military service, and requisitioned items already occupied two shelves in his bookcase. Calm and calculating, not lacking in joviality, a peasant's son, Monsieur Dennis, short-sighted, with chestnut eyes and a crew-cut, treated the great issues of concern to humanity with indifference. The question of whether, like his father, he will side with the ruling clericalists, or make contact with the liberal opposition, remained undecided: this will depend on the future, above all on his circle of legal clients. The German invasion struck De Baer like thunder, just as it did the whole of Leuven and Belgium. The Leuven student battalion was disbanded, and De Baer with several *copain* (pals) joined the Seventh Infantry Regiment, the same one that got a decoration at the Ijzer. The regiment was approximately equally divided between Flems and Walloons. The squad was commanded in the French language but, overwhelmingly, the Flemish peasants did not understand other languages, only their own dialect. When giving orders the commanding officer usually shouted, *Traduisez!* (Translate!). One of the Flemish junior officers then translated. During the campaigns, anxiety and the common danger brought the Flems and Walloons closely together, and they felt themselves to be Belgians *tout court* (just Belgians).

They had to put on their packs and move against the enemy. When De Baer realized that it was a serious business, he was seized with indignation. How on earth? By what right? His first thought was: a year lost at university! In the first days, he didn't seriously consider that Belgium could suffer, although he was organically patriotic and love for the homeland was deeply set in his bones. He had never harboured any enmity to the Germans, but had more immediate sympathy towards the French, thanks to a common language. Nevertheless, if they had asked him to become a Frenchman he would have been astonished. *Mais non, par exemple* (absolutely not) - I'd rather be Dutch if it came to it, despite the past! The fighting started. German lancers crossed the border and three army Corps approached Liège. De Baer was at this time in the Second Division depot. He had no involvement in the operations at Liège or Halen. At Halen there was a mixed squad of cyclist-riflemen, King's grenadiers and Queen's guards. De Baer's Seventh Infantry Regiment only received its baptism near Aarschot ... Belgium felt like a fishing boat caught between two dreadnoughts, closing in for mortal combat. At once, all questions of world politics confronted the Belgians, as they involved the fate of their country. Was it possible to let the Germans through Belgium? This thought occurred to no-one, apart from small commercial and industrial circles, directly dependent on German capital. For the peasantry and the petty bourgeoisie the issue was quite clear: the Germans cannot be let in. Not because it was prohibited by international treaty, but because the German army, having entered Belgium, was unlikely to want to leave. In addition, the army would take and despoil everything in its path. You must resist. They pinned their hopes almost exclusively on France and sincerely believed that the fate of Belgium would be resolved in two to three weeks of war. Echoes of the French mood in the first period dominated sentiment in Belgium. In the depot of the Second Division, they eagerly pounced on the news from Paris and repeated that the Germans would soon be thrown out, and they would be entering Berlin with the French.

The battle at Aarschot, the first battle in which our friend De Baer took part, seemed to him now like a fog. The town was occupied by the Germans without a fight, and the Seventh Infantry Regiment had to dislodge them. The enemy was in the minority, but defended stubbornly, confident that, in the end, they would win out. Shooting went on in the streets and houses, the population who had not managed to escape earlier hid in cellars. They took house by house, sometimes floor by floor. De Baer heard the persistent whistling of bullets around him, he fired a lot, but without aiming, and does not know whether killed or wounded even one German. Partly, he was hampered by short-sightedness. From the window of a one-story house in the outskirts, De Baer was hailed by Dubois, a soldier he knew from another company, an undertaker from Leuven, a well-known activist from the clerical party. De Baer glanced into the house and saw something horrible: on top of the blankets, on a wooden bed, lay a girl in the blood-stained remains of a shirt, both breasts had been cut off and there was a gaping wound in the lower abdomen. The girl was dead ... It was the most terrible thing that De Baer saw with his own eyes during the war, and he saw a lot ... They withdrew from Aarschot having suffered relatively small losses, but soon had to retreat in front of fresh enemy forces. When there were rumours about the withdrawal of the French, the ground began to tremble under them. The mood had irrevocably changed from the days, when, despite the looming threatening events, the soldiers in the Depot, joked and boasted: *a Berlin, a Berlin, patati patata!* (to Berlin, to Berlin, blah! blah! blah!) After Geest, Halen and Aarschot, the mood of the Seventh Infantry was deeply fractured. It became clear that the matter was much more serious than it had seemed at first.

From Aarschot they retreated to Leuven, which still did not anticipate the fate awaiting it. The Government, after remaining in Leuven for several days, moved on September 18th to Antwerp. Near Leuven, they had to hold up the offensive of three German Corps. On the first day, the 7th Infantry was assigned for a bayonet attack. A bashful young lieutenant made a short speech to his sections in a breaking voice. They moved in small groups, clinging to the ground, stumbling and clumsy from fear and tension. When they had moved far enough forward so that the enemy was clearly visible, the captain gave the command, and the bugler, a musician from a Brussels night Café, sounded the attack. They ran forward, *pas gymnastique* (with an athletic stride), gradually becoming intoxicated. Enemy bullets were already devastating their ranks, but they hardly noticed. The bugler blew continuously. Two hundred meters remained before the enemy line. *Hourra, hourra, vive le roi!* (Hurrah, hurrah, long live the King!)... Suddenly there is a river, or rather a big creek, three meters wide. Everyone stopped in their tracks, unable to believe their eyes. It turned out that the way forward was blocked. They were in a real trap. Beyond the river, a hundred steps away, the Germans in grey, lying on their stomachs, fired continuously. They were forced to lie down as well. The order was given to retreat - in the open, under constant fire. The Seventh Infantry lost a lot in this operation while retiring into the wood, and there were many slightly wounded. Ronday, a tall, stooping, taciturn officer, went grey as stone. "Mon commandant - the little shoemaker Jacob cried pitifully, I've been shot in the arm". He kept repeating the same thing several times, increasingly piteously. *Fichez-moi la paix* (leave off) - the officer finally answered, not looking at him - about your bullet in the arm, I've got two. Jacob immediately stopped whimpering. From then on he was one of the most fearless soldiers in the regiment. To this ordeal was soon added another. When moving to a new position in the woods surrounding Leuven, the regiment suddenly came under fire. Bullets were whistling at head height. From where? There was terrible confusion. "They're ours - Belgian!" the captain shouted suddenly. They rushed toward the shots, got as far as the edge of the wood and came upon the Germans. Horrified, they ran back into the forest. In the ranks, the word "treason" was passed around.

They spent three days in the Leuven woods, three days of constant fighting, moving from place to place. Most, including De Baer, fired at random, but some began to excel in shooting live targets. Sergeant Renken, a red-haired man with predatory jaw, a great marksman, boasted that he hid in foliage in a tree, fired 47 shots and brought down 47 Germans. Looking into his eyes, they believed him.

The enemy pressed forward, and quitting Leuven, they had to retreat further north to Antwerp. They spent a few weeks in billets, carrying out exercises and waiting for orders. The Seventh Infantry did not take part in the operation near Malin. In early October, it was transferred to Antwerp and put in the front line trenches. De Baer did not remember the date. He kept a detailed diary of events throughout the campaign, but during the panic-stricken flight from Lombardsijde dropped his pack, together with his diary, on the road. It was a terrible day! -actually, not a day, but half an hour ... but more about that later.

It became clear that in the further development of events it was inevitable that Belgium was doomed, and that the German army would go over her like a steam roller. An inexpressible, stifling hatred, a hatred of prostrate impotence, rose in their hearts and choked them. In these conditions, was it not surprising that the *franc-tireur* (civilians who took up arms) appeared, desperate madmen, who gave vent to their hatred by firing from behind curtains? In clerical Leuven they didn't defend the Jesuits, they shot them, taking vengeance on Belgium, as the country in Europe that had welcomed them the most. During the retreat, Dubois, the Leuven undertaker, often said to the peasants he came across along the way that they should take their guns down from the wall, since the Germans were on their heels ... *"Faites les boire le bouillon d'onze heures!* " (make it hot for them!)... Feelings of hatred deepened, as new facts from the epic of the German invasion, and new rumours about German atrocities, were absorbed. There were several occasions when an officer, with revolver in hand, had to defend a group of prisoners.

In the Antwerp trenches the Seventh Infantry first learned the true meaning of artillery. They were completely used to small arms fire, and sitting in the trenches, didn't give it any attention. They also thought that the Germans were bad shots. More dangerous was shrapnel: it exploded above them and shards found their way into the trench. But worst of all were the grenades. If they fell in the trench they tore down the concrete lining, making it into a lethal projectile. On the site of an explosion there was a mixture of concrete, clay and mangled human bodies. The mood in the trenches was oppressive - a mood of impending doom. Treating with exaggerated contempt the German infantry, they felt completely powerlessness before the German artillery. After the heroic defence of Liège, which soon took in people's minds a legendary outline, they had hoped that Namur, a stronger fortress, would hold out for several weeks. However, it fell in two days. As far as Antwerp was concerned, they were initially convinced that the fortress was impregnable. But by pulling out of the first line of fortifications, the soldiers made the unmistakable statement that to the roar of the German guns, Belgium had no answer. Since the Belgian artillery was made by Krupp, the firm conviction arose that in fulfilling the requirements of the General Staff, Krupp provided Belgium with low-grade material. It was passed on by word of mouth that many of the shells in Antwerp were filled with sawdust. Alarming rumours contributed to some tragic episodes. At the forts of Wavre and Saint Catherine, the lines were held for several days by the Sixth Regiment. The Seventh came to replace them. When the first company approached the trenches there was the familiar vzz-vzz sound. The first to fall, just a few steps from De-Baer, was M., the same officer who got two bullets in the arm near Leuven, this time the bullet entered and exited through the top of the forehead. It turned out that the trench was occupied by Germans. How did that happen? No one knew. Again they were talking about treason. British troops were expected. They arrived when the Belgian troops had already left the first line of trenches. The position of the fortress was hopeless, and this hopelessness was catastrophically shown in the city which, despite the alarm, which approached despair, existed up to the last moment in the inertia of an "impregnable fortress". In the hours when the fortress was surrendering, the town was in chaos.

The Seventh Infantry passed through Antwerp, going from south to north. It was October 8th. There was no doubt that the fortress was lost. All the food warehouses were wide open, and whoever came along was given whatever and as much as they liked. It was an overcast, but not a cold autumn day. Tens of thousands of soldiers went past: in their correct companies, in mixed groups or alone. Some, running from street to street searching for their company or their friends, took the time to go into food stores, and seized more than they were able to carry away or needed, and then gave it to the people or just threw it away to lighten their load. The stream of the retreating army mingled on the streets with a maelstrom of people, reduced to the last degree of despair. Some shops lowered their shutters, in others, the doors remained open, although there was no one behind the counter. Many thousands were leaving the city, grabbing a few belongings, women were rushing along, holding the hands of children and dragging others by the arm. An old woman, wailing loudly, pushed a wheelchair with a paralysed old man. Crying children ran between the ranks of soldiers looking for their parents. Mothers nursing their infants, pregnant women, maddened by fear, grabbed officers' sleeves and asked what to do. A police official, pale as chalk, tried to reassure them. Someone running through the square with their hands in the air, screamed that the Germans had entered the city. There was other news from the northern districts that a hundred thousand strong British army had appeared, or that the British fleet had entered the mouth of the Schelde estuary. The fear that the city would become the place where two huge armies met directly face to face, made the mad fire burn even brighter. Soldiers passed through the town, trying not to look around. "Colonel, shouted a grizzled, clean shaven old man from the door of his small shop, holding the hand of a boy of seven, you are leaving us to the mercy of the Germans!". The Colonel, who was sitting on a horse, silently rode on. De Baer slowly walked along beside his corporal. He already knew about the fate of Leuven and saw in it a reflection of the fate of Belgium and his own destiny. Everything is destroyed, all plans, customs, hopes ... As a lawyer, he remembered that the gun - *ultima ratio regum* - is the last argument of kings. Only now he truly understood the meaning of this saying. The German "argument" turned out to be stronger.

Stretched out over several kilometres, the Belgian army moved over the Schelde river, from the south bank to the north, on a bridge six to seven hundred metres long, newly thrown across. It was not a retreat, but a terrible final exit. The field army, together with the Antwerp garrison, the entire military strength of Belgium, had left Antwerp, the strongest fortress in the country, the last bastion of national independence ... When they destroyed the makeshift bridge, it seemed like they had forever renounced contact with the abandoned country. The day was overcast, with occasional fine but cold rain, the road was almost dry. They walked quickly, not talking, not looking back and wondering about the reason for the march. "It's all over, thought De Baer - it's all over. Leuven is destroyed, Antwerp has fallen, Brussels is occupied by the Germans. I don't know if my parents are alive, the precious dessert grapes from my father's greenhouse requisitioned, probably for officers of the German army". In vain, Dennis had studied Belgian law for three and a half years. Now, German law will be established in Belgium. Guns - the last argument of kings.

On the road, the captain of the first company requisitioned several carts, onto which they piled up their backpacks. It was easier to walk with two *poods* (1 *pood* is 16.3 kg) less on their backs. They still went quickly, in silence, without songs or jokes, shifting their rifles from one shoulder to the other. There was discordancy in the ranks, but no disorder. Sometimes swearing could be heard from under a moustache, or vague threatening gestures were made. After every hour a whistle sounded. They stopped, took their packs from the carts, sat on them, then rested for five minutes. On the whistle they got up and again walked for an hour. Where To? No one knew, no one pondered over it: anyway, there was already no way back. The junior officers walked alongside without giving commands or words of encouragement. The regimental banner was carried in the car next to the Colonel, who was riding a horse. They did not stop in the Flemish villages along the way, and barely talked to the people, as if they were in a foreign country. They didn't cook any food, but fed themselves from what was taken from the food stores in Antwerp. They walked all day, all night and then until noon - thirty-six hours without rest or sleep. On the first night, nerves were on edge so no-one felt tired. It seemed that their legs, freed from conscious control, moved themselves, and that this could go on indefinitely. On the second morning they felt tired. On the soles of their feet there were sores and chapping, most boots were bloody, and many walked with a limp. So passed the 100 km to Zelzate, a railway station on the Dutch border. The 7th Infantry left behind the first part of the Belgian epic.

II

The army walked for thirty-six hours from Antwerp to Zelzate. There the Seventh Infantry entrained. De Baer went into a carriage, lay down on the floor and barely managed to throw off his pack before he fell asleep. He was woken up in Ostend and taken to a billet in some guest-house. He was in a dead sleep all night, and could hardly wake up in the morning. The regiment again took to the field. They walked all day, feeling the pain in all their muscles after the great retreat. In the evening they came to the Ijzer. A new chapter was opening up in the bloody epic.

At the same time as the advanced detachments of Belgian troops were approaching the Ijzer from the west, the Germans came up to the canalised river from the east. The soldiers felt that their entire reserves of energy had already been used up in the battles and campaigns at Aarschot, Leuven and Antwerp and that their exit from these fortresses was the end of an era in their lives. And yet it was necessary to start all over again: the Germans were on the other side of the river. The officers said: "don't lose heart, we will be relieved by the evening. You only need to hold off the enemy until the arrival of the allies". But the evening arrived, and no one came. In this way, twelve expectant nights went by. The Belgian army, i.e. all that remained of it at the time, not less than 50 thousand men, was held on the Ijzer, under a constant onslaught of enemy fire.

De Baer aged physically during this period. He was never hurt by a bullet, shrapnel or by grenades, to which he felt a particular antipathy. It seemed amazing, and from time to time, especially after a good, sound sleep, he felt his arms and legs with rejoicing. But in fact, over De Baer only the ineluctable law of statistics operated. In every war there is a known number of soldiers who remain unscathed, who don't get a scratch. De Baer was apparently one of them.

The first eight days on the Ijzer were relatively easy, especially when compared with the last four. Artillery kept the Germans at a distance of several kilometres from the river. The Germans were waiting for more heavy guns for the opening of the offensive. The Belgian troops were digging trenches and settling down in them. De Baer has its own way of digging a personal trench, to which he attached great importance. The rains came, the earth went soft, and the soldiers were submerged in the mud even more.

On the third day of being encamped on the Ijzer, De Baer was returning in the evening to his "apartment" from work in the trench, sweaty, covered in mud, with pick and spade over his shoulder and a pack on his back. At the entrance to the second line trench, someone stopped him.

– Are you De Baer?

The student didn't see immediately through his dirty glasses who was there.

– Yes, I ... I, *Mon Colonel.*

– You were a law student?

– Yes, *Mon Colonel.*

– In the final year?
– Yes, *Mon Colonel.*
– So that's fixed ... Tomorrow we will convene a military court. There are thirteen accused. ... You'll be the defending counsel.

De Baer was stunned. How? Defence counsel in a military court? He had never in his life defended anyone in court. And besides, he hadn't met the thirteen accused and he didn't know the case at all, but the court was tomorrow morning ...

– It's nothing - his Colonel reassured him - we don't have a free officer, and you can familiarise yourself with the cases at the trial. So, tomorrow at nine o'clock in the village, in the headquarters building.
– Yes, *Mon colonel.*

De Baer, despite his fatigue, slept anxiously that night, just like before exams. The next day he scraped off as much dirt from himself as he could, washed more thoroughly than usual his face and hands, which had long ceased to resemble the hands of a student, and went to court.

All thirteen of the accused were Belgian soldiers, in cases of violation of discipline. Some faced the death penalty. De Baer took his place feeling as if he were the fourteenth defendant. But soon his usual prudence helped him not only to calm down, but to find what position he, as a soldier, could adopt between the prosecuting officers and the accused soldiers, so as not complicate his life in the future too much. The rapporteur stated in a few minutes the essence of each case, and from this De Baer found his material for questioning the few witnesses and for his speech for the defence. One of the accused was acquitted, it was the Fleming Eckhout, son of a wealthy peasant, a rustic, taciturn lad, accused of disobeying the red-haired Sergeant Renken, the same one who boasted that from the top of a tree he shot forty seven Germans, one after the other. The most perilous was the position of a gunner, who the Lieutenant threatened with the death penalty. Not putting himself forward too much, De Baer, thanks to the witnesses, helped the defendant to show that the Lieutenant maliciously and persistently persecuted him. The accused received the minimum sentence of three years hard labour. But there were two of the accused who De Baer himself was ready to sentence to death. These were two sentries who left their posts in sight of the enemy and went to sleep in a trench. The defence counsel immediately put himself in the position of a soldier, who, due to the action of the sentries, wakes up under a German bayonet. .... At twelve o'clock the Court concluded. The Colonel patted the defence counsel on the shoulder and then sent him two pairs of warm underwear. It was Dennis De Baer's first lawyer's fee.

On the ninth day, at dawn, an unprecedented attack began, even for this war. The Germans decided to take the Ijzer at any cost. They went forward in massive columns, straight at the Belgians, who opened fire with all barrels in their possession, especially the *mitrailleuse* (machine guns). When locusts, crossing a river, fall in hundreds of thousands, millions, layer upon layer, until they form a bridge, then this is already beyond the realm of biology, it is a mechanical process. And so it was here. It seemed from the Belgian trenches, that the German move forward under constant fire had in fact nothing tragic about it, because it was no longer human. Every German soldier in grey experienced the offensive in his own way, he mentally said goodbye to relatives, prayed to what he believed in, but collectively they created an impersonal grey mass, paving the way with their dead bodies. The *mitrailleuse* worked, scattering death in a semi-circle, just like a giant horizontal pendulum describing a deadly arc, wiping out row after row. From the first line, ten or so survived, as well as those the pendulum had not managed to scythe down in the second row, and in the place of the fallen and over their corpses went a new, fresh, grey mass. No matter how methodically the mitrailleuse worked - tra-ta-ta-ta, they could not get into every cranny of the approaching columns, and the human mass continued to approach the river. It was only when it came up quite close to the opposite bank, that it temporarily flashed into De Baer's mind that these are people, and that they came over the bodies of other people. But once they were very close, it turned out that they were direct enemies, who you had to save yourself from by wiping them out.

The Seventh Infantry remained on the Ijzer for four more days, and it was the most dangerous time in the whole campaign. The regiment was stationed at Saint Georges, a small settlement on the left bank. On the other side of the Ijzer, the Germans, under fire, began to dig trenches. The enemies stood face to face, separated by the ribbon of the canal. The section of the first company, which was under De Baer, was positioned no farther than a meter from the water. Both sides kept a sharp lookout for each other. Anyone whose head bobbed above the parapet, immediately fell to the bottom of the trench. There was bitterness in both camps. The Germans hung on with their teeth to the positions they had paid so dearly for. The Belgians were afraid of losing theirs. Once, they managed to see a grenade fall in the German trench, throwing utensils and soldiers clothes two or three metres in the air in a cloud of sand and smoke.... The Belgian trench began to applaud.

It was very hard with food. Once a day, in the evening, they had to send someone out for it, and they were never sure he would get back. It was even worse with water.

The Ijzer was right there, but there were a lot of dead bodies, human waste and blood in it. There was no choice though, they had to drink from the river. De Baer's trench had the advantage that it was possible to throw a bucket directly over the parapet, fixed to a bayonet. When the bucket was raised up, it was often hit by an enemy bullet. But the Germans in general kept their reputations as poor shots.

It was cold at night and few had blankets. One of the few was Eckhout, the same one De Baer had defended in court. After he was acquitted, he was transferred to the first section, so that he did not come across Sergeant Renken. Once in the same trench as De Baer, the Fleming firmly attached himself to his lawyer. At night when sleeping, sitting curled up in the cubby holes in the sides of the trench, waiting in suspense for a German attack across the river, Eckhout always carefully covered his defence counsel with a half-warm blanket. In De Baer's trench there were always many victims. The Lieutenant fell first: entering the trench whistling cheerfully, he was hit in the temple with shrapnel from a grenade. On the same day, another grenade exploded in the middle of the trench and killed twelve people. They lay right there for hours. At night they were carried away and buried next to the trench. They used the pits created by the enemy shells, adapting them for human bodies with their spades - the same spades that were used to dig the trench. The work was distressing, it was pity for the dead. But pity for the wounded, grief for those killed, disgust at the foul water - all these feelings and sensations were smothered, because over all of them the will for self-preservation dominated. So they survived twelve days on the Ijzer. At dawn on the last day De Baer slept heavily and erratically in a sitting position, completely stiff, wrapped in a blanket with his Flemish friend. Suddenly in his sleep, he heard the familiar disturbing sound of shrapnel, just like the noise of a carriage without rubber tyres, and then boom, an explosion in the air, and then in an instant - vzzz ... shrapnel projectiles ... Another instant, and some kind of electrical impulse went down his right side. De Baer woke up and in horror pushed something away with his hands. To his right, under the blanket was the motionless body of Eckhout: a bullet had entered between the eyes, leaving a neat hole.

In the evening of that day the Seventh Infantry was finally relieved and sent to rest in the nearest village. In front of them was two or three weeks of security, sleep and hot meals. But it didn't work out like that. That night the Germans opened a formidable offensive movement across the river, throwing bridges over, and knocking the Belgians out of the trenches - all, as before, at the cost of continuous indifference to self-destruction, and an avalanche of human flesh moved westward, as far as the railway line which runs through Newport and Ramskapelle. Among the Belgian soldiers who had been thrown back, there was confusion, bordering on panic. It was necessary to replenish the front lines. But the reserves of the Belgian army were still the same. The

Seventh Infantry was again called up to the hottest position. It had managed to spend only one night at its new encampment after twelve days of continuous combat.

Something twitched in the chest of the Leuven student. Will he be one of those who, according to the statistics, return home unharmed and healthy after all the danger of war? The first battalion entrenched along the railroad line a kilometre from the hostile positions. De Baer again dug a protective niche according to his "system", to which he attached great importance. Trench life began again, with the cold, dirt and constant danger. On the third day De Baer was again appointed defence counsel. They tried three Germans and one Belgian and the four men were sentenced to death. When the twelve soldiers fired, the Germans fell, but the Belgian remained. The officer looked into the faces of soldiers, said nothing and killed the condemned man with a revolver.

On the fifth day they noticed ominous animation in the German lines - they were preparing a new onslaught. The first battalion, which had suffered great losses and was deadly tired, was relieved by the second. De Baer relished the long rest and again was bitterly mistaken. The Belgian line could not withstand the onslaught. At the decisive moment the second battalion did not have enough ammunition. The Germans crossed over the railway and took the important station of Ramskapelle. The first battalion, not having had time to wash or to dry out, was moved from its billet and sent into the attack at Ramskapelle. After all their ordeals and especially after the abortive leave, they vented their anger in this attack, where both sides fought with equal fury.

The Germans wavered along the length of the railway line itself. A few soldiers of the first battalion, among whom stood out the tall, stout, student of medicine, Camus, caught up with a fleeing group of the enemy. They stopped and a young German soldier, slender with a light fuzz on his upper lip, turned his bayonet against Camus. The medical student completely forgot all the techniques they had taught him for protection from a bayonet, and began grabbing the bayonet in his right hand, while holding his rifle in the left. At the same moment a bayonet was stuck in his palm and went right through. Camus barely had time to shout out with a shrill scream, when the little shoemaker with short legs, Jacob, the one who was slightly wounded at Leuven, thrust his bayonet into the belly of the young German. The young man fell with a groan but his gun with the bayonet was still in Camus's hand. The student screamed, slowly taking his hand off the bayonet. Two other Germans fought to the last, with the desperation of the cornered. One of them grabbed his rifle by the barrel and swung it like a club, completely smashing Jacob's lower jaw on the side. De Baer ran to help, but it was too late. Both enemy stragglers had already been stabbed to death.

The Germans had spent too much nervous energy in the mad offensive against the Ijzer and now began to retreat, evacuating Ramskapelle and the railway line. By that time, the Belgians already had come into contact with the left wing of the French army. In Ramskapelle the Seventh Infantry joined together with a French infantry regiment, and both remained there all day. In the evening, the "Seventh" was finally sent to recuperate at Koksijde. On the fifth day, it was withdrawn to Furneaux, less than an hour away, where there was a solemn ceremony: the award of a decoration to the regimental banner. The Seventh Infantry, cleaned up and straightened out, was lined up on the square. De Baer was standing a long way from the banner. He saw the tall figure of the King, but, however hard he tried, could not hear the words of his speech. The King fixed to the banner the Order of Excellence, and the band played the anthems of the allies and the *"Brabant"* (The Belgian national anthem). The mood was festive in the town. The Seventh Infantry with its honours came back from Furneaux to rest in Koksijde. But doom was gathering over the regiment.

Their rest was again short-lived. Just the next day an order came to pull out within an hour. The regiment was sent Newport. A decisive operation lay ahead, the expulsion of the Germans from Lombardsijde. The military authorities decided that for such an audacious enterprise the Seventh Infantry, who had only just received the Order of Excellence, were best suited for the task. But it turned out otherwise. From Newport, they crossed the Ijzer and then a river parallel to it, and under the cover of its bluff, went in single file next to the water, in the direction of Lombardsijde. Crouching as low as possible and clinging to the bank, so as not to slip into the water, they went eight hundred metres. Coming up to the footbridge spanning the river at Lombardsijde, they came out from under cover for the attack. But the air on three sides was immediately filled with familiar sounds. Vzzz ... vzzz ... The soldiers later said that they were exploding bullets, because apart from the insinuating vzzz ... they heard a clak-clak as well ... it was clear, the regiment was surrounded on three sides. There was chaos. The first to fall was Major N, then the red-haired Sergeant Renken and many, many others. The shout went up: *Sauve qui peut!* (every man for himself!) which signalled the final panic. The Germans were attacking from three sides - the Seventh Infantry was trapped. *Sauve qui peut!* Some gave up, others tried to flee. Most rushed back under cover of the bank by the water. Among them was De Baer. But now there was no time to move in single file. Running up against each other while escaping, they fell into the water. There was continuous fire above them - vzzz... vzzz ... clack-clack...- maybe these were the bullets hitting the water. De Baer realized that running any further under the bank meant he was bound to perish. In two jumps, he was on top, in the open on the road, and directly under enemy fire, he ran to the footbridge. Someone ran up behind and jabbed him in the shoulder, De Baer fell heavily onto the path. A strap on his pack broke, and his glasses described an arc in the air and smashed onto the path. Getting up, De Baer threw the pack off his back and keeping the rifle in his hands, ran on without his glasses. Everything was swimming in his myopic gaze. Someone ran to head him off. Vzzz .. vzzz..., "but the Germans are bad shots". De Baer never for a moment lost sight of his goal. How well he remembered those moments! Here he is on the bridge, in the most dangerous place, in full view of the Germans. Holy statistics, save me! They rescued him. De Baer in a few jumps was on the other side of the river and without drawing breath ran to Newport....

In this ill-fated operation the Seventh Infantry lost 1,000 killed, drowned, wounded, but mainly captured. The general state of the regiment was fundamentally undermined. "Who led us into an ambush?" After all their ordeals, exploits - and celebrations at Furneaux - such a deadly collapse! The remnants of the regiment were sent to recuperate at De Panne. There the regiment was reorganized and after a prolonged stay was sent to the trenches near Ramskapelle. It was already late autumn, it rained continuously and floods threatened from the north. The 7th Infantry spent fifteen days in the trenches at Ramskapelle. De Baer was all that time without his glasses, and the world seemed shapeless to him. Fortunately, the regiment didn't once come into contact with the enemy during this time. It then went back to rest in De Panne. The regimental doctor sent De Baer to the hospital in Calais to get new glasses. But instead, the Leuven student was acknowledged to be too short-sighted for military service and released entirely. It was early January...

For De Baer it was the start of a new life. He wandered about without any ties, almost in rags, always hungry, giving up hope. Three weeks later he got a job as a waiter in one of the restaurants in Calais. And the Seventh Infantry continued to add to its story in those two Flanders Departments still under the authority of the Belgian Government sitting in Le Havre ...

Calais, February 16, 1915

Note

1. Part I published in *Kieven Thought* No 63, March 4th 1915, Part II in No 65, March 6th 1915. First translation from Russian.

The Trench[1]

I

Regardless of the heavy artillery, airplanes, telephones and planners, in this long drawn-out and stationary war, the hand grenades of Gustav-Adolph and the field engineering of Vauban are supplemented, according to an apt formulation in *Figaro*, with customs and pictures of military life, almost copied from the Siege of Troy.[2]

The trench extends from Dunkirk to Belfort. It crawls through the dunes of Flanders, the black thread then twists along the chalky spaces of Champagne, and meanders into the pine forests of the Vosges - a line of 800 kilometres. In this trench, the French army is hidden, trying to stand its ground. The French trench is not temporary - put up in different places and at different moments in the course of the struggle. It is a crucial boundary, the slightest movement of which, to one side or the other, is paid for in incalculable victims.

When the artillery in the sector subsides, there is nothing to indicate this is a battlefield. The area is deserted and lifeless. No soldiers, no guns. There is nothing to say that this small space contains the hidden lives of several thousand people. In their gloomy lairs they sit, sleep, eat, dress wounds, die; along the passages or in neighbouring pockets they move from place to place; on the surface, nothing can be seen or heard. Trench warfare is above all a particularly bloody game of hide and seek. This war of moles is so contrary to "the Gallic temperament" ...

– "A disgusting dump of a dungeon imposed on us by the Germans,"- even the French press sometimes complains now. But the originality of the national genius has worn off in another area: the French are sitting in trenches, as are the Germans, the Russians and the Italians. The trench has proved more potent than the "Gallic temperament".

The trench has been there for many months. If it had been known it would be necessary to live in it for so long, it would have been organised differently. Well, maybe there wouldn't have been enough heart to build it at all. But it was assumed that the trenches were only support points for a new movement forward. They built them up gradually: they reinforced the pillars, raised the parapets, improved and camouflaged the embrasures. Equipping them with anything that came to hand: a tree trunk, a box, sacks of earth, the greatcoat of a slain German ... The soldiers have almost forgotten to regard the trench as a temporary shelter. They speak of it as they did before about the border of France, only their conception of the front is far more concrete, after a year of struggle and suffering.

Life in the trenches stands midway between life in the "apartments" in the second line (cantonnements) and direct military confrontation, The trench puts the soldier in close contact with the enemy. Even when there are no incursions, the enemy presence is felt all the time, in the form of constant artillery and rifle fire; German voices and the sound of underground works are often heard, and sometimes an enemy's head rises above the parapet. In the evening, a song rings out and often, especially in the heat of an exchange of fire, or before an attack - swearing and cursing.

The trench immediately straightens out fresh soldiers. They have only just moved from the camp to the immediate war danger zone, where, over and around them, bullets are squealing. They suddenly tighten up, their energy focused on self-preservation. They strive more closely to attach themselves to their unit, more strictly observing standards of discipline and order, which they now regard not as alien, imposed and arbitrary, but as reasonable methods to protect their life from danger. Discipline establishes itself without any friction.

"Till this moment, says a French officer about the first baptism of fire of his battalion, I rebuked my soldiers for indifference and a lack of understanding of the importance of the situation. But on this night, their eyes were burning, full of attention. They listened to my orders, as to the voice of the Oracle, endorsing them with "yes, yes", repeated several times in a low voice" ... What made them do this? A common purpose? No. It was the immediate danger, the first contact with a German unit. "Once, says an observant non-commissioned officer, we moved out to relieve the men in the trenches. We had to go five kilometres. The men almost waddled along, chatting. Suddenly a shell fell to the side of us. The squad immediately stopped and for a few seconds was stunned, then moved forward in superb order and in silence, with an easy tempo that demonstrated a switch to a rhythmic marching step from the normal one".

Change-over in the trenches normally takes place at night. Fresh troops sometimes only see in the morning how close they are to the enemy and what kind of danger they were in on their way to the trench. They are amazed how they managed to avoid death in these circumstances, and in hindsight feel a sharp jolt of fear. Immediately, the soldiers are filled with gratitude towards their guardian-cave, watching bullets hit the parapet or whistling over their heads. The instinct of self-preservation at first completely overwhelms all others that are subordinate to the instinct to survive, including the need for comfort. If for external visitors to the trench, life is monstrous, in the eyes of the soldier the trench compensates for its dark side, by giving him a safe haven.

Later, a great familiarity sets in with regard to the trench. The soldier not only looks at it as protection, but also as living accommodation. At the same time he becomes more demanding, begining his new placement after every break with criticism of the state the lodging was left in by his predecessor. On the way to the trench, they already start guessing to what extent the other shift has cleared away the traces of its stay. This is fully revealed in a case quoted to us by L. M. Lahy, of the tensions that exist between the various clans. Woe-betide Gunners if they occupy an Infantry trench: there are then no end of taunts from the grimy foot-soldiers.

Having settled in, the soldier wants to orientate himself. He seeks to determine the position of his trench in relation to the enemy, the proximity with other trenches and communications with the rear. After the first tide of fear, he tends to overestimate how safe he is. Young soldiers aim to stick their heads above the parapet to look around, and only the shouts of more experienced comrades makes them keep in line. Shift after shift, the soldiers fit in, learn what they can and can't do, get used to the terrain, learn to distinguish every bump on it, because behind every tussock lies mortal danger. The slightest change in the deceptive surface no longer escapes them. But the battle-field is deadly and monotonous. The terrible razor of war has passed along the line of trenches hundreds of times, rendering it smooth. This trench was previously in the forest. The shells tore out and broke most of the trees. The others were then eliminated by humans and used for interior fittings of the trench. A tree near the trench is dangerous. After hitting it, the shell explodes prematurely and gives the enemy an opportunity to adjust his sights more accurately. A bullet strikes the trunk, and the ricochet kills. In the end, around each trench which has been under fire for a long time, and that means all the current French trenches, a grim desert is formed, and through the loopholes the eye always rests on the same landscape of destruction. "We are back in the trenches, a Russian volunteer says in a letter, and again in the centre of our positions, that is on top of mines and under "krapujo", as our soldiers call mortar fire. Forty five to fifty meters from us are the Germans. All around in the valleys and on the mountains, there is richly alluring greenery, but in our accursed positions not a single live bush: stone, ploughed-up earth, shell holes and dust. And it was a town. There's nothing left ... And so it is everywhere".

II

Some hundred metres, sometimes much less, separates the enemy trenches. The enemies almost never see each other, but they follow the barely perceptible signs of everything that happens. They know all the routines, even the most minor habits of the enemy trench. The need to adapt to an invisible enemy makes it necessary to recognize them by their actions. And what is the main activity of the enemy? Shooting. Methodologically, a shot is fired from the loophole every five minutes. This is the pedant, firing without rancour, without any specific intent to harm. Another shoots to no purpose from the parapet, not aiming and not counting the cartridges. A third reduces his obligations to a minimum, his credo the most composed, he sends a bullet as a rare gift. A fourth fires at random, trying to kill with a ricochet. Each has his own style and habit. This one is a dangerous and sure shot, on the look-out for every shadow, an undoubted sluggard or a sportsman, or a jester.... At the change-over these disappear, new ones appear and mutual adaptation and identification begins once more. Another change-over and old acquaintances are returning.

Sentries keep vigil at their posts. The others are busy with what? Who is dozing, sewing, writing ... Some are cleaning out the passage, others are playing cards. In the machine gunners' dug-out a jeweler is making rings, the copper and aluminium for which are supplied by German shells. All is quiet, almost peaceful. Meanwhile, the enemy is close, much closer than one might think. This trench was taken from the Germans. It is connected to the second line with a passage at right angles, which the Germans have now moved into. It is blocked half- way along with a wall made out of sacks of earth. On one side of the dividing wall is a French sentry, and on the other a German. So they stand there, on the watch for each others breathing. Both has a rifle between his knees, a grenade in hand, and a bag of grenades close by. The slightest threatening movement from the opposing party and the infernal music begins ...

The neighbouring enemies live a common life, experience the same events and have the same feelings. The enemy automatically adapts to the same clay or sand, also suffers from the same rain, chokes on the heat and breaths in the smell of a corpse, decomposing in the middle, between the two ditches. In the incessant struggle they imitate each other: periscope against periscope, grenade against grenade, telephone against telephone. They conduct mining operations against each other, equally uncertain who fate will first send flying up in the air.

But here's a surprise, unexpected in its naturalness. A June downpour bursts into the lives of the two trenches and drives the soldiers to the surface. "On June 10, another Russian volunteer writes from the front, we had a flooded trench. All the dugouts were flooded; the water was waist-deep, and on lower ground it was up to the throat. People were washed out onto the embankment. For the Germans it was the same story. As if by tacit agreement, neither side considered the possibility of opening fire on east targets. All that was allowed was an agreement for pumping out water. Food warming tins and buckets were pressed into service. The chain was started in full view of the Germans. The water level doesn't subside. We are looking for the cause. It turns out that the water is returning through mole-holes in the trench. Finally, it was put right, the water was pumped back into the field, and fire resumed"...

When a squad occupies the same trench for a long time and the enemy's fire does not cause too much devastation, then life in the trench carries on like in the depot or in the cantonnements: the squabbling, the jokes, the bullying resume, they are needed to fill the void of consciousness.

A striking expression of a closed mental life is the development of a special language: something that is observed in boarding houses, barracks and prisons. Well known facts and phenomena, new or old, appear before the soldiers, whose particular relevance, seen from the perspective in the trench, seems to require the incorporation of a new word. A number of these words have already spilled over from the trenches in everyday French and have come into the language. The latest levy of young soldiers, like a century ago, are called Marie-Louise, named after the Austrian Princess who became Empress of France and demanded from the Senate that the recruits of 1814 be named after her. While battle hardened soldiers are called poilus, elderly reservists with semi-ironic affection are called peperes, something like the word for Pop. The word marmite, a pot, is used to denote large enemy projectiles. 75 mm guns are called "Eugenia", and the bayonet has the slightly sweet name: "Rosalia".

Any extraneous labour is pushed aside that threatens to dislodge a weary uniform consciousness from the condition of unstable equilibrium to which it clings. The soldiers in the trenches appear to forget about their profession, rarely recall their family and mostly evade any minor manual work, which trench life leaves enough time for. Uncommon will-power or particularly favourable conditions are needed to take advantage of forced leisure time, or of any material that comes to hand, that could give an outlet for creative energy.

Here, in the trench, very little thought is given to general military tasks and, while it may seem a paradox, even less thought is given to the enemy. The enemy trench, which sends death in the form of a canon, flinging over murderous fire, will of course, always absorb the soldiers attention. But here the issue is not about Germany, not the plans of Emperor Wilhelm, or the German withdrawal, not about the historical enemy. It is about a piece of lead or cast iron bringing death, from which it is necessary to escape by sending iron and lead into the enemy trenches. They talk about the enemy with more animation when waiting to attack, or when they are preparing for it, but they speak about it in terms of physical confrontation.

The soldiers wait intently for letters, read them anxiously, but always remain unsatisfied. The letter arouses half-forgotten, strongly suppressed memories, thoughts and feelings and provokes unresolved anxiety about another world. But the trench now announces its presence, places itself in command, and the impression given by the letters is quickly wiped out. Enlarging the instinct of self-preservation, the trench inculcates an egotistical consciousness. When the poilus thinks about himself, he almost always hears his soul cry: "they're out there, and I'm here; I'm afraid for them, I will defend them, I can be killed".

After a year of war, soldiers began to be given four days leave from the front. With their units, they left the sector and then spread out to their home areas. Out of the carriage windows, the peasant soldiers eagerly look on the growing ears of corn and discuss the autumn tasks. The trench is left behind. Everyone is talking or thinking about their family, anticipating the affection of the meeting, worrying… A lot could change in a year. But in the family, in the home village or town the '*permissioners*'[3] (those released on a short leave), despite the joy of the meeting and the feeling of safety, do not feel at ease. Between them and the home environment there is not the former balance. The broken mental link is not restored immediately. A sense of dissatisfaction springs up, which can take a stormy or even tragic form. There were cases when the permissioner left before the end of the leave or shot his wife and himself. Four days pass quickly. In the carriage on the way back, the returning soldiers greet their comrades. They cursorily share their impressions of the leave. But their mind is already fixed on the trench. They talk about it, remember, anticipate. The closed environment again absorbs them mentally, before they are physically immersed in it.

Paris.

Notes

1. *Kievan Thought* September 20, 21, 1915. First translation from the Russian.
2. Swedish King, Gustav Adolf, (1594-1632) was credited with introducing new technology into military life, such as the grenade. Sebastian Vauban, (1633-1707), foremost military engineer of his day under French king, Louis XIV. Particular expert on seige warfare. Figaro is a reference to the French daily newspaper.
3. Trotsky uses the French slang term.

Psychological Enigmas of War[1]

For thirteen months Europe has been immersed in blood and flames. And perhaps the most surprising phenomenon of the war is that it has lasted for thirteen months and that humanity in Europe has endured. That generation of European intellectuals, raised in a culture of the most refined sensibilities, demonstrated by the art of "raw nerves",[2] now sits in the trenches with peasants and workers, soaked in the rain, burnt to a cinder by the sun, covered with lice and yet – they endure. How many prophets of doom have whined in our ears that the civilized world is heading towards physical degeneration? And meanwhile.... Oh, indeed, the young generation could find other more worthy ways to expend their energy, but it would be hopelessly blind not to see that the mainsprings of the new epoch – machines, electricity, automobiles, newspapers, the City – have imbued in humanity unprecedented energy and incredible stamina!

Undoubtedly, mankind entered this war stronger, more intrepid, more healthy than ever before. But if it came into the war like this, how will it leave it? How much creative energy will the war devour? To what extent will it weaken and deplete Europe? What changes will it make in the consciousness of our generation and what will grow imperceptibly to take its place? What feelings and consciousness will those who return from their trenches bring back? These questions are enigmas. As long as the matter concerns finance, industry and politics, prognosis, at least within general trends, is still possible. But it is infinitely more difficult to take into account those direct changes which the war engenders in the minds of modern humanity. However, it is completely clear that the present catastrophe will, for years, decades and centuries will radiate a bloody light which for future generations will illuminate their destiny, just as modern Europe, until yesterday, felt the light of the Great French Revolution and the Napoleonic Wars. And how minor are those events, separated from us by five quarter centuries, compared to those that we are now involved in or experiencing, and especially those which are approaching!

The human mind has a tendency to banality. As it slowly and reluctantly clambers to the summit of colossal events, it always unconsciously seeks, despite all the rhetoric, to lessen their significance, so as to more easily assimilate them. In general, among the many things that have suffered a terrible collapse in this war are human minds and this has led to false consciousness.

Still, with unprecedented clarity, human psychology has been shown to be a most conservative force: great events do not spring from our consciousness, but rather, events arise from a combination of the interaction and intersection of large objective historical forces, forcing our inflexible, lazy mind, hobbling and limping , to adapt to them. In this fact, so hurtful to the megalomania, which is our second nature, there cries out the current fate of the modern civilised nations, in the combined thunder of all the guns and rifles. War arrived, apart from and in opposition to, consciousness. It fell on it and subjugated, not only all material and social life with all its complexity, but also the spiritual experience of nations, separate social groups, small collectives and individuals, the feelings and thoughts of rulers and ruled, of military corps and convents, workers' organizations, universities, mothers and sweethearts. The war is not controlled by the conscious mind; it is the war that governs consciousness. So what changes will it make to it?

Current events have sharply posed a question about the degeneration that has occurred and is occurring in the minds of the flower of the European nations. The most vital and creative generations are now locked in an iron honeycomb of regiments, divisions and corps. They have begun a journey, by way of barracks, depots, camps and trenches, through all the stages which will take them to the centre of the conflict, to attack, advance, defend, retreat. Some will be struck from the list of the living, the path of others will lay through medical stations, field hospitals and convalescent homes, to return into society, blind, crippled, without arms or legs....

What internal psychological forces, what immediate experiences are pushing this human mass towards the most " inhuman" ordeal, where everything that was considered valuable is broken and destroyed: health, comfort, hygiene, order, the usual everyday relationships, friendships, professional responsibilities, and ultimately an unshakable moral order? What new psychological reflections will it provoke, what changes will this terrible bloody chaos, which has become the new order, bring in?

To sum up the process happening before our eyes, even in a most general and approximate way, is now extremely difficult, primarily because we ourselves, that is, all those among us who ask themselves such questions, are not disinterested observers of events, for whom the survival of nations, social groups and individuals are only raw material be subject to scientific analysis - and where besides are the scientific methods of mass psychology? - No, we are all, in one way or another, from one point of view or another, in the grip of events, from head to toe we are entirely at their mercy, and not only do we judge them, but immediately seek to turn our own opinions into a small factor in these events. From another angle, the raw material is too immense, too diverse, and can never be collected in a genuinely "raw" form. It is always transformed on its journey, at least into semi-finished material. In crude terms, modern society can be divided into two unequal parts: the direct participants in the battle and the audience passionately gripped by it. Between the two there is a narrow layer of intermediaries; professionals, military observers and chroniclers. Direct participants in the military events have the least ability of any to remain calm and objective as narrators of what they are going through. It needs utterly extraordinary mental endurance and a high level of psychological self-control, to consciously capture in memory experiences tested in the most critical moments of battle, when vital forces are strained to the ultimate degree towards immediate self-preservation, in order to give these experiences, in an unembellished and untouched form, a general direction. It is a well-established fact that direct participants in battle, after going through many meetings and interviews, in an attempt to establish in memory what happened to them, do not give a true picture, but a new, far more sophisticated approach, in which there are elements of creativity, imagination, rumour, conjecture, hypnosis and finally painting, could play a huge role.

On the other hand, the professional intermediaries between the army and the country, the war correspondents, provide material, often very graphic and interesting, but in most cases of little psychological reliability. Above all, because they observe from afar: further pretensions of the correspondents, at least on the French front, are absolutely not allowed [Correspondents were prevented from going near the front lines- Ed]. But even in those cases when they do manage to see things as they really are, only the most superficial details are imprinted on the retina, one incidental particle of the huge process that constitutes war. However, the phenomena that we are interested in now, by their very nature cannot be imprinted on even the most sensitive retina: they are psychological processes, emotional development and the metamorphosis of consciousness.

Correspondents themselves are not solely observers, in fact, least of all observers, they are more often enemies of objective observation: they are passionate actors in the drama, the nation's conduit between the front-line and society. They perform a known political function: to maintain at a high level the general state of the combatants, encouraging their own nation and terrorizing their opponents. Their reports, not only in their judgements and conclusions, but above all their factual accounts, are always painted in definite colours. And perhaps not just, because of conscious bias, but due to natural selection, a particular attitude of mind is generated. Finally, interest in the psychology of war arose much later than interest in the war itself. If the mind, as we have said, is always sluggish and lagging behind events, it is not surprising that the greatest interest in psychology arises later than interest in objective historical events, with their dynamic and dramatic nature.

However, given persistence and the necessary prerequisites for scientific research, it is possible that some work has already appeared, that shows not inferior results in the field of the psychology of war. Direct contact with soldiers and officers in the field gives extremely valuable material, not yet subject to internal and external processing. When a soldier has spent several days in a trench under a constant barrage of enemy artillery or after an attack, his thoughts and feelings still remaining in the immediate past, his psyche depleted of resources and with insufficient energy to embellish and decorate his experiences with inventions and speculations, then he will give, maybe a meagre, but in its immediacy, a true account of what he has just thought and felt. Needless to say, the work here will retain its relevance in its critical separation of the wheat from the chaff...

To a certain extent, a reliable source can also be the letters of soldiers that are written directly at the front, over a long period of time to the same person, to whom the soldier is not dressing things up or posing. This is especially true, perhaps, in the first period of the war, before a military suntan has been acquired on the body or the mind, bringing its formulaic phraseology and hackneyed trench routine. The events of the war are to such an extent extraordinary, and throw the consciousness of the soldier out of balance to such a degree, that it is hard in his old lexicon to find the right words to give an account of what has happened in front of his eyes and in his mind. And this difficulty, the poverty of words to express shattering new experiences, typically engulfs the soldier in the first period, so that he has neither the strength, the time nor the inclination to amplify and embellish his experiences.

In short, if you combine research methods, if you bring into them the control of unflinching criticism, material free from overlapping, fresh data obtained from third parties, if, based on them and arming oneself with redoubled scepticism and valuable material from secondary sources, i.e. newspapers and books, you can come close to very interesting and significant conclusions about the psychology of war.

Paris.

Notes

1. *Kievan Thought*, September 11 1915. First translation from Russian. A few sentences are reproduced in Chapter VIII of 'The Prophet Armed, Trotsky: 1879-1921', by Isaac Deutscher, OUP, London, 1970.
2. This could be a reference to the Expressionist School, perhaps having Edvard Munch's 1895 painting 'The Scream' in mind.
3. The literal translation is 'pseudo-dominant claim on consciousness'.